Reproducible Activities

Nonfiction
Reading Comprehension

Grades 7-8

D1608520

By
Linda Piazza

Cover Design by
Matthew Van Zomeren

Inside Illustrations by
Don O'Connor

Published by Instructional Fair • TS Denison
an imprint of

McGraw-Hill
Children's Publishing

About the Author
A summa cum laude graduate of the University of Houston's nationally acclaimed creative writing program, Linda Piazza has written numerous articles and stories for the educational market. She also authored another reading comprehension activity book previously published by Instructional Fair. She is also the author of five young-adult novels published in the United States and Germany. She and her husband live in Houston, Texas.

Credits
Author: Linda Piazza
Inside Illustrations: Don O'Connor
Cover Design: Jeff Van Kanegan
Project Director/Editor: Jerry Aten
Editor: Sharon Thompson
Graphic Layout: Jeff Van Kanegan and
                Sharon Thompson

McGraw-Hill
Children's Publishing

A Division of The **McGraw·Hill** *Companies*

Published by Instructional Fair • TS Denison
An imprint of McGraw-Hill Children's Publishing
Copyright © 2002 McGraw-Hill Children's Publishing

Send all inquiries to:
McGraw-Hill Children's Publishing
3195 Wilson Drive NW
Grand Rapids, Michigan 49544

Nonfiction Reading Comprehension—grades 7–8
ISBN: 0-7424-0221-5

2 3 4 5 6 7 8 9 PHXBK 07 06 05 04 03

Table of Contents

Name _____

Plan It

Imagine that the manager of your local grocery store gives you a chance for a weekend job. To test your ability to follow directions, the manager hands you a floor plan of the store's west wing. The manager also gives you a list of tasks to complete. Study the task list and floor plan, then number the store sections in the order you will visit them. Circles have been provided for your use.

The Manager's Directions

1. Pick up returned bottles in the bottle storage room and wheel them to the truck-loading ramp.
2. Wait there for delivery of meat, milk, ice cream, and bread products.
3. Store ice cream before it melts. Next, deliver meat to the butchers. Then bring bread to bakery storage area.
4. Go to the produce area and help trim lettuce.
5. Report to the employee lounge after you have completed all these tasks.

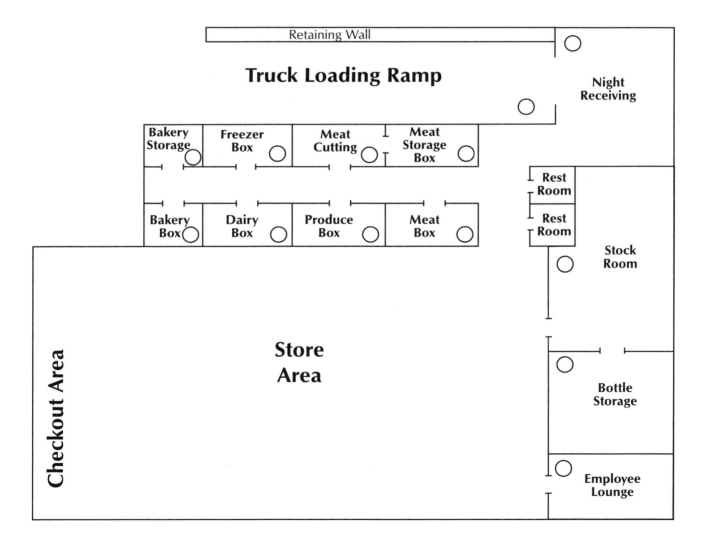

Name _____

Cheap Thrills

At your school's library, you pick up a book with a screaming, monstrous face on the cover. You will need your parents' permission to check out this book. Some parents in your school district do not want their children reading horror books.

Other generations battled their parents over reading matter, too. From the mid-nineteenth century to the early twentieth, novelists wrote dime novels, penny dreadfuls, and shilling shockers. As their names indicate, these novels cost pennies and were sold in the United States and Britain. Often hastily written, they featured lots of action and sometimes lots of blood and gore, too. That is why penny dreadfuls were also known as *bloods*.

Many people objected to the blood and gore in these novels. Some objected to the second-rate writing that many featured. These novels had their defenders, however. The English writer G. K. Chesterton pointed out that these novels dealt with moral issues of evil versus good, even if they did it in a sensational manner. Today's horror novels often do the same.

That does not mean that all such books make appropriate reading for students or for adults, either. Some prove as dreadful as the penny dreadfuls. Perhaps each should be evaluated on its own merits.

Write your answers in the space below. Base those answers on what you read in "Cheap Thrills" and what you might know from your own experience.

---

1. Name three ways that dime novels and similar books compare to today's paperback horror series books. _____

   _____

   _____

2. Compare or contrast two concerns about the dime novels to the concerns about today's paperback horror series books.

   _____

   _____

3. What does the author of "Cheap Thrills" hope to persuade readers to do?

   _____

Name _____

Say What?

President Kennedy once traveled to Berlin, Germany. The Berliners had suffered after World War II. President Kennedy wanted to show the bond he felt with them. He practiced saying *I am a citizen of Berlin* in German to create that bond. When the time came to speak, instead of saying *Ich bin Berliner,* as the correct translation would read, he intoned the words *Ich bin eine Berliner.* The addition of the word *eine* changed his sentence. His new sentence translated into *I am a cream-filled pastry!* Despite his political blooper, the Berliners loved him for trying.

Read the following bloopers. They are funny because the politicians goofed and used the wrong word or phrase. These wrong words are printed in bold type. Think about the context of the statement the politician was making. What word should the politician have used instead? You will find suggestions inside the parentheses that follow each sentence. Help the politician out by underlining the correct word or words. Use a dictionary, if needed.

1. George W. Bush, Presidential Candidate, talking about people who did not take his abilities seriously enough: They **misunderestimated** me. (misunderstood, underestimated)

2. Al Gore, Vice President: A zebra doesn't change its **spots**. (stripes, mind)

3. Thomas M. Menino, Mayor of Boston: The [school] principals deserve the right to install **mental detectors** in their schools. (mental inspectors, metal detectors)

4. Gib Lewis, Texas House Speaker: This is **unparalyzed** in the state's history. (unpasteurized, unparalleled)

5. Gib Lewis, Texas House Speaker: I want to thank each and every one of you for having **extinguished** yourselves in this season. (distinguished, exterminated)

6. John King, New Hampshire Governor: I am privileged to speak at this **millstone** in the history of this college. (milestone, load)

7. George Bush, Presidential Candidate: I like meeting people, my fellow citizens, I like **interfacing** with them. (interfering, interacting)

8. Dan Quayle, Vice President: One word sums up probably the responsibility of any vice president, and that one word is **"to be prepared**." (to be ready, preparedness)

9. Dan Quayle, Vice President: It's wonderful to be here in the great **state** of Chicago. (city, country)

The Generals of the Sierra Nevada

Below you will find three article openings. Each opening introduces the same topic—the ages of the famous Sierra Nevada sequoia trees. The openings sound different, because the author wrote each for a different audience and a different purpose. The author uses a different voice in each. Read the three openings, thinking about the author's voice and how that might connect to the author's purpose. Fill in the blanks below, choosing from the following possible answers: to inform professionals, to entertain young people while informing them, to persuade citizens to take action.

Opening 1
The sequoias in the famed Sierra Nevada are shrinking. In age, that is.

Opening 2
To assess the impact of global warming and other environmental changes on the Sierra Nevada, the U.S. Geological Survey initiated the Sierra Nevada Global Change Research Program. To fulfill the parameters of this program, it became necessary to accurately compute the ages of the sequoias, most notably the General Grant and the General Sherman.

Opening 3
Two aging generals need your help. Still proud, the two old men of the Sequoia National Park stand guard. Now they are threatened by the environmental havoc we humans have created. Nate Stephenson of the U.S. Geological Survey's Sierra Nevada Global Change Research Program tells us that these trees are not as old as we once thought. Still, they have guarded this forest for two millennia. When you have learned how long they have lived, you will want to do what you can to protect them.

1. The voice of opening 1 hints that the author's purpose is _____
   _____ .

2. The voice of opening 2 hints that the author's purpose is _____
   _____ .

3. The voice of opening 3 hints that the author's purpose is _____
   _____ .

Write your answer.
4. Which opening would be the most likely to appear in a scientific journal? _____
   _____

5. Which opening would be the most likely to appear in a pop-up on a Saturday
   morning television program for teens? _____

6. Which opening would be the most likely to appear in a letter asking for contributions
   to a fund to stop global warming? _____

Tsunami Dangers

Summarizing can help you organize the main points of a passage. It may help you to remember those points. A summary consists of a brief description of the main points. Read the following passage about tsunamis, noticing the most important points the author makes. Then answer the questions that follow.

The wave rose up taller than a four-story building. It crashed into the shore, wiping out villages along four miles of the coastline. More than 2,000 people died. This disaster happened in Papua New Guinea, but it could happen next in the United States.

Great sea waves, or *tsunamis*, usually follow earthquakes or volcanic eruptions. An earthquake preceded the tsunami in Papua New Guinea, but something about that tsunami puzzled scientists. They calculated that the tsunami should have hit the shoreline ten minutes sooner than it did. Something other than the earthquake must have caused it.

That something turned out to be an undersea landslide. Terraces of loose sediment had formed where rivers emptied into the ocean. The earthquake started a landslide. That loose sediment cascaded down with the speed of a snow avalanche.

Similar terraces of loose sediment line the Southern California and mid-Atlantic coasts. Earthquakes or eruptions of gas pockets could cause avalanches in those areas, too. An underwater landslide on the mid-Atlantic coastline could send 18-foot waves as far inland as Washington, D.C. More people live along the California and mid-Atlantic coastlines than live along Papua New Guinea's. That means that more people would be in danger from a tsunami. The results could be even more disastrous than in Papua New Guinea.

Currently, scientists know of no way to protect people living along these shorelines. Seismographs can detect earthquakes but not undersea landslides. Even if scientists could detect the landslides, residents of coastline communities would not have time to evacuate before a tsunami hit. The solution to the danger lies in learning to predict the landslides before they happen, giving residents of these shorelines time to evacuate.

1. Write a single sentence that summarizes the damage done by the tsunami that hit Papua New Guinea.

   _____

2. Write a single sentence that summarizes the possible causes of a tsunami.

   _____

3. Why do scientists feel that residents along the Southern California and mid-Atlantic coasts face danger from tsunamis? Write a summary in two or three sentences.

   _____

   _____

   _____

4. Why do scientists need to predict when undersea landslides might occur along a coastline? Write a single sentence that summarizes this need.

   _____

5. Write two to four sentences that summarize the most important points of the article.

   _____

   _____

   _____

Name _____

Chewy Doesn't Go to Yellowstone

Your family plans a trip to Yellowstone National Park. You want to take your dog, Chewy. He is a big, athletic dog, and he will love the outdoors. You are surprised when a friend tells you about Yellowstone's rules. Review the rules your friend recounts: Rangers will not allow pets anywhere in the backcountry or on trails or boardwalks. Owners cannot leave pets unattended or leashed to any object. Owners have to clean up after their dogs.

Before your friend dashes off to his soccer game, he tells you that the rules are meant to protect the park, visitors to the park, wildlife, and your pet. He does not have time to tell you more.

Draw your own conclusions about the prohibitions against pets.

1. List two ways pets might disturb the natural area or the wildlife at Yellowstone.

   _____

   _____

2. List one way pets might disturb other park visitors.

   _____

3. List two ways pets might become endangered in a natural park.

   _____

   _____

Answer P for possible or NP for not possible.

_____ 4. Since all mammals can contract rabies, visiting pets might spread rabies or other illnesses to park wildlife or pick up illnesses from them.

_____ 5. An escaped pet might have difficulty surviving in the wild.

Name _____

(Not) Just the Facts

Journalists fill the pages of newspapers with facts. Journalists also include quotations in those articles. Those quotations sometimes reveal facts and sometimes reveal opinions. Newspapers also include advertisements. Those advertisements might include facts or offer opinions about services or products. A single online issue of the *Washington Post* included the following statements. Read them and write F for fact or O for opinion. Remember that a fact can be proved to be wrong but still be a fact.

_____ 1. In March, the Park Service banned . . . jet skis from 66 of 87 parks, recreational areas, and seashores.

_____ 2. Home Hunter: Washington, D.C.'s best place to find a home.

_____ 3. 12 Years Online

_____ 4. Study Aims to Pinpoint How Acupuncture Works

_____ 5. Millions of Americans have tried the ancient Chinese treatment [acupuncture].

_____ 6. Few alternative therapies had been . . . tested in clinical trials.

_____ 7. Researchers hope to enroll 570 people older than 50.

_____ 8. School-based anti-smoking programs have had little effect in smoking prevention.

_____ 9. *washingtonpost.com*: Your continual source of political intelligence.

_____10. 24 MB Smart Media: As low as $109.95.

_____11. Your neighborhood school may be the best choice.

_____12. University of Maryland: Quality. Discovery. Impact.

_____13. An educator must be well-organized and prepared.

_____14. Expect snow and ice-glazed roads.

_____15. Four traffic deaths were blamed on the storm in New Mexico.

_____16. Heavy rains may turn to ice later in the day.

Have a Bug Feast

Entomologists study insects. To organize their studies, they classify or categorize insects into different groups, based on shared characteristics. Classifying items or ideas can help you organize information, too. As you read this article about insects, think about the different ways you might classify the insects that are discussed.

Professor Roger Gold asks Texas A&M students to eat bugs. He whips the insects into tasty dishes and encourages students and staff to dig in. Other universities push bug food, too.

Maybe you do not think steamed crickets or baked mealworms sound tasty. How about rootworm beetle dip or banana worm bread, each featuring chopped or ground-up insects? Ohio State University's entomology department offers recipes for those two.

While some insects prove toxic and should not be eaten, most insects offer many nutritional advantages. Although high in protein, they contain little fat. They provide many vitamins and a variety of tastes and textures. Some boast sweet, nutty flavors; some might be crunchy and tangy; and some might taste like bacon or other familiar foods. They are plentiful, cheap, and easy to harvest.

Moreover, humans have been eating insects throughout history. Many cultures still consume them. In Asia, some people roast giant water bugs and eat them whole. Some Mexican stores stock cans of fried grasshoppers. Ground-up ants might show up as spreads on bread in Colombia.

Ground-up insects might show up in the United States, too. Flours, spreads, and chopped, frozen, and canned vegetables inevitably contain tiny bits of ground-up insects. Without knowing it, you and other Americans unintentionally eat one to two pounds of insects each year.

Don't worry. Remember all those proteins and vitamins. Also, entomologists insist that insects are cleaner than other animals. Better a few ground-up insects in your food than more pesticide residues, entomologists also say.

Eat up.

Imagine that entomologists set up two classifications titled "Insects with a Social Structure" and "Insects with Wings." Where would the entomologist include bees? Bees have wings. Bees also live in colonies with a social structure. Each bee contributes to the hive. Bees could fit under either classification. Those two classifications would not be mutually exclusive. An insect that belonged in one classification would not necessarily be excluded from the other one. When scientists set up classifications, they try to assign mutually exclusive classifications.

Below you will find sets of classifications, based on material in "Have a Bug Feast." Write ME for mutually exclusive classifications and NME for the classifications that are not mutually exclusive.

_____ 1. *Poisonous Insects* and *Nonpoisonous Insects*

_____ 2. *Edible Insects* and *Inedible Insects*

_____ 3. *Insects with Sweet, Nutty Flavors* and *Low-fat Insects*

_____ 4. *Flours, Spreads, and Chopped Vegetables* and *Colombian Spreads for Bread*

5. Below you will find two groups of items. Think about how the items in each group compare to each other, and how they differ from the items in the other group. Then write titles for each group of items, making certain that you choose mutually exclusive titles.

Title A: _____
Flour
Chopped frozen vegetables
Chopped canned vegetables

Title B: _____
Banana worm bread
Roasted water bugs
Cans of fried grasshoppers

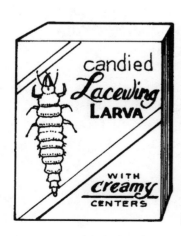

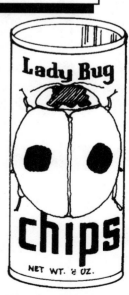

Name _____

My Most Embarrassing Moment

Below you will find an account of an embarrassing moment experienced by a real-life teen. Humorous writing sometimes depends on tension and surprise to create a humorous effect. Read this account, noticing the prose structure the author uses. Then answer the questions which follow.

My friends and I had just put down our trays at a local hamburger place when I spotted this guy sitting a few tables away. I'd seen him a few times in the hall at school, but I had never talked to him. Here was my chance to make him remember me. I made sure I got a seat facing him. As I sat down, I made eye contact. I picked up my drink, still making eye contact. I lifted my drink, still making eye contact. I accidentally stuck the straw up my nostril, still making eye contact.

He burst out laughing. From then on, he laughed every time he passed me in the hall. He remembered me, all right.

1. The author starts this teen's tale by setting the scene and telling why it was important that the girl make a good impression. In your opinion, why did the author want you to imagine the setting? _____

   _____

2. In your opinion, why did the author want you to know how important this moment was to the girl who relates her experience? _____

   _____

3. The author repeats the phrase "still making eye contact" three times. In your opinion, why does the author use repetition? _____

   _____

4. What effect does the author create when things turn out differently than readers might have expected? _____

Name _____

Spacey Diets

Imagine that your school has the honor of ordering supplies for three astronauts' meals on an upcoming spaceflight. You're in charge of lunch on the first day.

NASA's dietician uses Venn diagrams like the one below to organize the foods needed for each meal. The dietician draws three circles, one for each astronaut. If all three astronauts wanted a lunch item, the dietician listed that item in the area where all circles overlapped. If only two astronauts wanted an item, the dietician listed that item in the area where the two astronauts' circles overlapped. If only one astronaut wanted an item, the dietician listed that item in that astronaut's circle, in an area that did not overlap with another astronaut's circle.

Now complete this form by listing the number of orders of each food item needed:

_____ tropical punch

_____ lemonade

_____ orange-pineapple drink

_____ dried beef

_____ shrimp cocktail

_____ carrot sticks

_____ peach ambrosia

_____ beef steak

_____ macaroni and cheese

_____ potatoes au gratin

_____ broccoli au gratin

_____ green beans with mushrooms

_____ green beans and broccoli

_____ butter cookies

_____ chocolate pudding

_____ tapioca pudding

_____ candy-coated peanuts

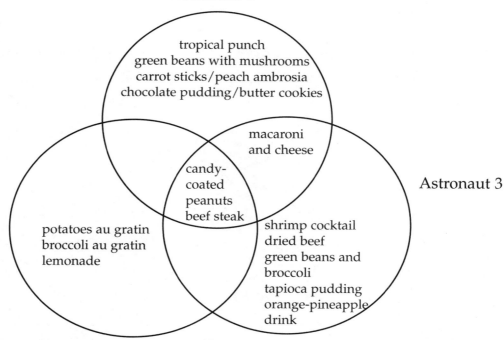

Astronaut 1

tropical punch
green beans with mushrooms
carrot sticks/peach ambrosia
chocolate pudding/butter cookies

macaroni
and cheese

candy-
coated
peanuts
beef steak

Astronaut 2

Astronaut 3

potatoes au gratin
broccoli au gratin
lemonade

shrimp cocktail
dried beef
green beans and
broccoli
tapioca pudding
orange-pineapple
drink

Ocean Solutions

As you read this article about global warming, notice which of the statements are facts and which are the opinions of the scientists.

It is many years in the future. Deep in the dark green ocean water, an ice-like rock sits on the ocean floor. That rock and others like it have saved the planet from global warming.

At least, that is what some scientists hope. The rock does not exist yet, but global warming does. Excess carbon dioxide causes global warming. Scientists search for ways to remove excess carbon dioxide. They imagine piping it deep under the ocean. The deep-water pressure would transform the carbon dioxide gas into a liquid that would freeze into icelike chunks in the cold ocean depths.

Another novel method of ridding the planet of carbon dioxide involves dumping iron into the ocean. Tiny plants called plankton grow faster in the presence of iron. Plankton absorbs carbon dioxide. Some scientists believe that when the tiny, waterborne plants die, they might sink to the bottom of the ocean, carrying the excess carbon dioxide with them.

Not all solutions to the global warming problem involve the ocean, of course. Scientists explore many possibilities for storing or removing excess carbon dioxide. More importantly, they are studying ways to limit the production of carbon dioxide in the future.

Name _____

On this page, you will solve a word-search puzzle and find one fact and one opinion about plankton and carbon dioxide. Follow the directions below:

1. Search for the words written below the puzzle. When you locate each word in the puzzle, mark out the letters that make up the word.

2. Now that you have found all those words, the leftover letters form a hidden message.

   (You will have six letters left over.) Write the hidden message here: _____
   _____

3. Now unscramble the original word list to form another sentence about plankton. Write that sentence here. _____

4. One of the two sentences you formed was a fact and one was an opinion. Circle the fact.

T	H	E	D	Y	P	I	N	G
P	L	A	N	T	L	S	W	O
S	R	E	T	S	A	F	U	L
D	E	C	A	I	N	R	R	Y
E	X	K	R	C	K	E	S	S
C	A	O	A	R	T	B	O	N
D	N	I	O	M	O	X	I	D
E	T	O	T	H	N	E	O	C
W	O	R	G	E	A	N	F	L
O	O	R	X	V	A	C	K	Y

FASTER   GROW
IRON   MAKES
PLANKTON

Name _____

Teasing Out the Answers

Nonfiction sometimes entertains. Even entertaining nonfiction can require reading strategies. You might need to slow your reading rate, reread, or take notes. Below you will find three brainteasers from *www.brain-teaser.com*. Solving them might require all of those reading tactics and more! Pay attention to details and have fun.

Brainteaser 1:
A family gathers for Thanksgiving. The family group consists of 1 grandfather, 1 grandmother, 2 fathers, 2 mothers, 4 children, 3 grandchildren, 1 brother, 2 sisters, 2 sons, 2 daughters, 1 father-in-law, 1 mother-in-law, and 1 daughter-in-law. The family fits comfortably around a dining room table that seats eight or fewer people. How is that possible?

Notes: _____

_____

Solution: _____

_____

Brainteaser 2:
If today is Monday, what is the day after the day before the day before tomorrow? Hint: Break this puzzle into several steps, rephrasing the question as you go. For example, the day before tomorrow is today. As a first step to solving the puzzle, rephrase the question to read *If today is Monday, what is the day after the day before today?*

Notes: _____

_____

Solution: _____

_____

Brainteaser 3:
If the puzzle you solved before you solved the puzzle you solved after you solved the puzzle you solved before you solved this one was harder than the puzzle you solved after you solved the puzzle you solved before you solved this one, was the puzzle you solved before you solved this one harder than this one? Answer yes or no. Hint: Break this brainteaser into steps and rephrase the question, just as you did on Brainteaser 2.

Notes: _____

_____

Solution: _____

_____

Name _____

Spend, Spend, Spend

You will find a promotion for a SpendBigBukz card on this page. This fake promotion employs many of the tactics used in actual promotions to teens and adults. In actual ads, advertisers set time limits, promise popularity or other accomplishments, offer free gifts, and use other tactics. As you read about the SpendBigBukz prepaid card, notice the tactics used in this marketing campaign.

You're the best! You know it and we do, too. To prove it, we're putting your photo on your very own prepaid card. Sign up this week and we'll even load your card with $25.00 for your first purchase.

Buy what you want with your own SpendBigBukz Prepaid Card. Your parents preload the account and you spend the money. The card works just like cash. What could be easier? Plus, you get cash back for every purchase you make. The more you spend, the more you earn!

Be the best! Get a SpendBigBukz Prepaid Card now.

Write your answers.
1. Imagine that the SpendBigBukz company uses this ad as an online promotion. List at least two types of sites where you would expect this banner ad to appear.

   _____

2. Circle each instance when the advertisement uses the words *spend, buy,* or *cash.*

3. What does the advertisement promise to teens who sign up within one week? Name at least two other promises made to teens who sign up at any time._____

   _____

4. The advertisement does not mention whether the SpendBigBukz company charges a yearly fee for the card. List two other questions you or your parents might want answered before you signed up for this card. _____

   _____

Tramp Art

Read the following selection, looking for specific details and sensory images that help you visualize tramp art.

A man stood outside a general store sometime in the mid-1930s. He unwrapped the tattered flour sack from around a wooden object. Holding up the object for inspection to the first store patron who appeared, he asked, "Could you use a picture frame?"

The frame was an example of tramp art. The man had fashioned the frame from thin layers of wood. Tiny V-shaped notches decorated the edges of each quarter-inch layer. He cut each layer narrower than the one beneath it, and then stacked them. Glue held the layers together, and a dab of yellow paint dotted each notch. The notches and thin layers created an intricate, geometrical design.

This folk-art form probably began in Europe where fathers taught their sons the craft. In America, most tramp art was created during the Depression. Desperate men known as tramps roamed the country, vainly looking for work. Some made objects to sell. Poverty forced the artists to scavenge wood and paint for their projects. Cigar boxes and fruit crates often furnished the wood. Many tramp artists created picture frames, but some also built bigger objects such as desks and chests. Some artists smoothed and burnished their projects to a deep luster, and some also painted them when they could scavenge paint.

A group of formerly homeless men recently revived this folk-art tradition. Working together, these men have been luckier than many of the tramp artists of the Depression era. They have built a business, funding homes for themselves. When someone comes knocking at their doors, maybe they will remember the desperate tramp artists of old and buy what is being sold.

Name _____

Draw one of the objects described, as you visualized it when you were reading the selection.

Snoopy Snakes

Authors often use a three-part structure when writing nonfiction. The opening captures readers' interest and also introduces the topic. The author might write a question, a surprising statement, or an anecdote or scene to capture readers' interest. The body of the article expands on the topic. It introduces details that support the main idea. The conclusion wraps up the article. Sometimes the conclusion echoes the article's beginning. It might conclude the scene introduced in the opening. It might answer a question asked in the opening or make another surprising statement to return to the mood created by the article's opening. Read the article. Put a set of brackets around each of its three parts.

These snakes don't bite. They don't have fangs. They're robot snakes.

Several researchers around the world are building snake robots. These robots include several sections that can be fitted together. Although the different versions of snake robots may operate in slightly different ways, sensors in each section usually detect that section's position. All the sensors send information to a single unit that coordinates movements. It functions as a brain would. In one model, the tail section includes a battery, so that the snake does not have to be tethered to a cord. Head sections often include optical sensors.

Those optical sensors do more than an actual snake's eyes do. They send information back to the people operating the snake. That's why these snakes make ideal inspection tools.

They can slither into tight tubes and send information back to human operators. That ability might make them useful to people in some industries. Researchers hope that they'll slither across alien landscapes, too, sending information about other planets back to Earth.

What's next? Ant robots? Actually, they already exist.

In this article, the conclusion does not mention snakes, yet still echoes the opening. How would you describe the way that the conclusion returns to the mood of the opening?

_____

_____

_____

Name _____

Dreaming Up a Good Grade

Read the title of the page and the first paragraph of the article below. Decide what main idea the article will discuss. Then scan the article quickly for specific details that will help support that main idea. Circle those details.

You've got a big test tomorrow. You decide to stay up all night studying, but that's a big mistake. If you're going to do your best on that test, you need to dream about it.

Two studies indicate that dreams help you sort out and remember new information or tasks. During a study in Belgium, volunteers watched symbols flash across a screen. The test required them to press the same symbol on a keyboard. Some volunteers worked on the test for several hours, slept, and then retook the test upon waking. They improved their scores. During the tests, scans of their brains highlighted the most active areas. Those same areas appeared most active during their dreams. Researchers believe that the volunteers practiced the test in their dreams and then stored what they learned.

A study by Dr. Robert Stickgold, a psychiatrist at Harvard Medical School, showed the same result. Volunteers played a computer game. Two thirds of those volunteers dreamed about the game. Stickgold concluded that dreams help people sort out new experiences and store them in long-term memory. His research included volunteers with damage to the hippocampus, a part of the brain that remembers what happens in the past. The people with damage to the hippocampus could not store the memories sorted out during their dreams. Although dreams do not originate in the hippocampus, that part of the brain apparently played a part in storing the memories.

These two research studies confirm what your mother always told you: you need a good night's sleep if you want to do your best.

Answer the following questions, relying only on the details you circled.

1. Some scientists believe that dreams help people remember new information or new tasks. How many studies supported this theory? _____

2. What is the name of the Harvard psychiatrist who conducted one of the studies?

   _____

3. What portion of volunteers in the Harvard study dreamed about the computer game?

   _____

4. What part of the brain stores memories? _____

Mathew Brady's Plan to End Warfare

Can inventions change history? The development of the cotton gin changed the landscape and economy of the American South. The article on this page discusses Mathew Brady and his efforts to change history. As you read this article, notice what caused Brady to think that he could change history. What effects did Brady hope to achieve and what caused him to fail or succeed?

Mathew Brady tried to end warfare for all time. He used a new, powerful weapon. He used a camera.

Brady opened his first photography studio in 1844. The images he produced were daguerreotypes, not the photographs he would later snap. Daguerreotypes recorded images on sheets of copper coated with silver. They required long exposures to produce the image. A person being photographed would have to stay perfectly still for three to fifteen minutes. That made daguerreotypes impractical for portraits. By 1855, though, Brady was advertising a new type of image that had just been invented: a photograph made on paper.

From the beginning of his career, Brady thought that photography could serve an important purpose. His images could create a record of national life. When the Civil War broke out, he wanted to document the war. Although his costs were prohibitive and his friends discouraged him, he assembled a corps of photographers. He also bought photographs from others returning from the field. His efforts culminated in an 1862 display of photographs made after the Battle of Antietam. The bloodshed shocked the exhibit's visitors, most of whom had never known what warfare was like.

Brady did not stop warfare, of course. He did not even earn enough money to pay for his venture. After the Civil War, people lost interest in his chronicle of the war. He found few buyers for the photographs. He went bankrupt. Years after the war, Congress bought his collection, but he earned only enough money to pay the debts that had built up while he assembled the collection.

Still, Brady recorded one of the most important episodes in American history. In doing so, he created the first photo-documentation of a war. Perhaps, some day, another photo documentation of another war will accomplish Brady's goal.

Answer the following questions about cause and effect. Base your answers on what you read in "Mathew Brady's Plan to End Warfare" and what you might already have known about Mathew Brady and his time.

1. What might have caused the people in daguerreotype portraits to look stiff and unnatural? _____

2. What new technology caused Mathew Brady to think that he could change history?

   _____

3. What effect did the end of the Civil War have on Mathew Brady's personal finances? Why? _____

4. Name two causes behind the creation of the first photo-documentation of a war.

   _____

   _____

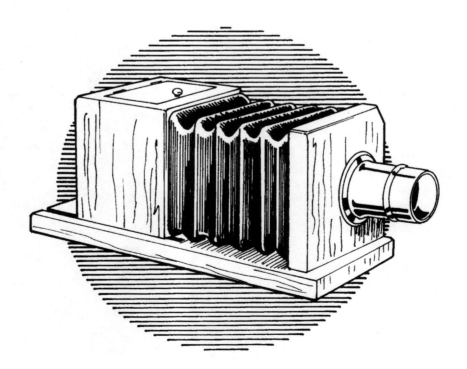

Driving Distracted

Taking notes can help you organize and remember new information. A concept map provides a great way to take notes. Start with the main idea in a circle or box in the center. Then jot down important details or ideas in various spots around the circle or box. Connect related ideas with rays or lines.

A concept map has been started for you on the next page. Some ideas or details still need to be added. Read the article, noting how the details and ideas relate to one another. Notice what might be missing and fill in the details.

Ahead, you notice a car drifting across the road. "Mom," you say as you grab the cell phone. "I think there's a drunk driver up ahead." Just as you're dialing 911, you notice the driver ahead of you has a cell phone to his ear, too. He's not driving drunk. He's driving distracted.

It's going to get worse, the National Highway Traffic Safety Administration fears. Although cell phones, car televisions, and CD players have been with us for a while, some cars now offer new distractions. Those include on-board maps, fax machines, and even wireless access to the Internet. Already these devices contribute to about one fourth of the 6.3 million automobile crashes each year.

Voice-activated devices will help, some suggest. Still, voice activation won't eliminate the distractions of these devices. To ensure safety, some car manufacturers set up Internet access so that the car must be in park before devices can be engaged. Other manufacturers allow access any time. Some politicians believe that new laws must be passed, setting limits for when such devices can be used.

If they could only set limits for how many times your younger siblings could scream in the car, that would really lessen the distractions!

Fill in the missing details.

Their use contributes to ¼ of 6.3 million crashes each year.

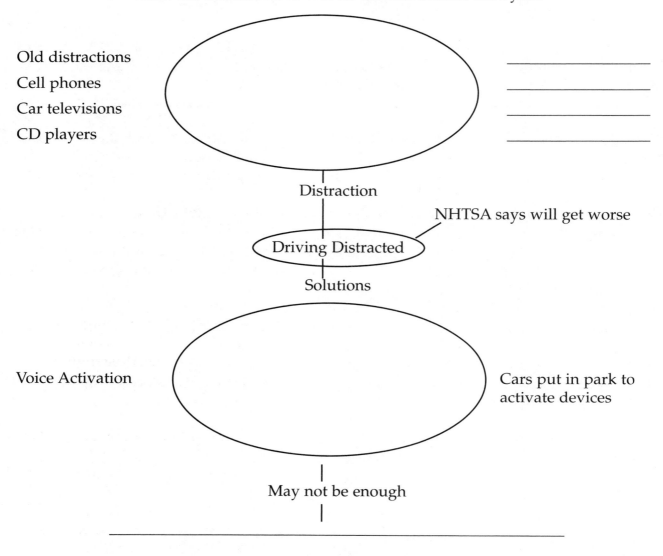

Old distractions
Cell phones
Car televisions
CD players

_____
_____
_____
_____

Distraction

Driving Distracted   NHTSA says will get worse

Solutions

Voice Activation   Cars put in park to activate devices

May not be enough

_____
_____

Name _____

A New Capitol for a New Nation

Similes compare two unlike things that share one element in common. A person who is as busy as a bee shares the bee's tendency to flit from one task to another. The words *like* and *as* sometimes signal the author's use of a simile. A metaphor also compares two unlike things, but a metaphor seldom uses the words *like* or *as*. A metaphor does not say something is like another thing; it says it is that other thing. A metaphor would not say that a person has a heart like gold, for example. It would say that person has a heart of gold. Read the following profile of William Thornton. Circle any similes or metaphors the author uses to make comparisons.

People call the United States a melting pot of immigrants. Perhaps it was fitting, then, that an immigrant designed the capitol building. The United States nourished the dreams of its immigrants. Perhaps it is also fitting that an untrained architect designed America's most important public building.

William Thornton was born in the British Virgin Islands in 1759. Educated to be a doctor, he traveled the world, arriving in the United States in 1787. He became a citizen a year later, but he was not finished with his travels. He was visiting his native country when he heard about a fascinating competition.

The new nation needed a capitol building. Thomas Jefferson and George Washington decided to hold a competition for the best design. Like its flag, this building would symbolize the new nation and the ideas that had formed it. Jefferson and Washington specified the dimensions of the new building but not the style. They wanted ideas from the people of the new country.

When traveling, Thornton had viewed many of the world's most important buildings. He was not an architect, but he was a Renaissance man who dreamed of designing buildings. His drawing revealed a classical design, one that would endure through the centuries.

His drawing arrived months after the competition ended, but that did not matter to Jefferson and Washington. They chose Thornton's design. An immigrant with no formal training in architecture had designed the capitol building for a nation of ambitious immigrants.

Write your answer. Many language experts think that too many people have used the melting-pot metaphor. They call it a tired or overused metaphor. Suggest another metaphor for the United States. Draw from the idea that many immigrants contributed to the country.

Name _____

The Capitol Building

Construction on the Capitol Building began in 1793. Construction ended with the installation of Thomas Crawford's bronze Statue of Freedom on the cupola of the dome. Although Jefferson and Washington chose William Thornton's design for the exterior, many architects supervised construction through the years that followed. Those architects changed and enlarged the original design.

Below you will find a copy of Thornton's original drawing and a drawing of the Capitol from the west front as it stands today. Study the two drawings, noting the similarities and differences. Write your answers.

1. Write two or three sentences that compare the two drawings, noting the similarities you see.

   _____

   _____

   _____

2. Write two or three sentences that contrast the two drawings, noting the differences you see.

   _____

   _____

   _____

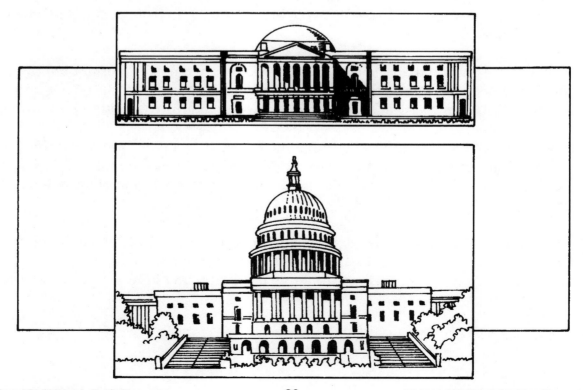

Name _____

Banana Vaccinations

Nonfiction sometimes offers information about planned developments in science or other areas. New developments do not always fulfill their promises. Theories may prove unworkable. As you read about new developments, pay attention to the supporting details the author offers. Does the author present only the advantages of this new development or does the author also mention potential drawbacks? Do you have enough information to make an informed judgment about the development?

This article discusses a researcher's attempts to modify bananas genetically so that they protect children against childhood illnesses. Start by writing your initial opinion of this plan. Do you think it might be workable? What advantages do you imagine this type of immunization might provide?

_____

_____

Now read the article, looking for details that either support or argue against your initial opinion. Notice whether the author provides enough details or instead makes broad statements without any supporting facts. Refine your initial opinion as you read.

It's time for a tetanus vaccination. The doctor comes in with something hidden behind her back. It's the needle, you think, but when she opens her hand, she's holding a slice of a banana. The banana has been biologically engineered to immunize you against tetanus.

No immunizing bananas exist yet, but researcher Charles Arntzen hopes they soon will. He doesn't worry too much about American children and their sore arms, though. He worries about children in third-world countries who die because they don't get immunizations. Tetanus kills 500,000 newborns a year across the world. An Associated Press article reports that about four million people, mostly children, die each year from tetanus and other illnesses that might be prevented by vaccination.

Why don't these countries vaccinate their children? Vaccinations prove too costly for poor nations. Some vaccinations require refrigeration, making it impossible to deliver them to hard-to-reach settlements. Even if those refrigerated vaccines could be delivered, they almost always require injections. Trained medical personnel must be available to immunize children. In poor countries, few people are trained for these procedures.

Arntzen realized that bananas grow in many of those countries where children need immunizations. He knew something about genetic modification of plants. Now he hopes to grow bananas with proteins that could cause those children to build up immunities to childhood illnesses.

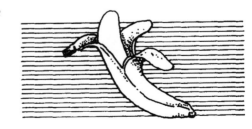

Arntzen needs to work out a few problems first. Bananas grow easily in many of these countries, but bananas prove harder to modify than other fruits and vegetables. Even if Arntzen does modify the bananas in the way he wants, he must make certain that the bananas deliver a consistent dosage. Too much of the proteins would cause the children to develop a tolerance for a disease, not an immunity to it. The modified banana trees would have to be kept separate from other trees and plants, so that not all plants would carry these properties. Financing the project continues to be a problem, too.

Arntzen has already produced potatoes that can immunize—if they are eaten raw. Cooking destroys the proteins. Still, he's making progress. Perhaps when your younger siblings go to a doctor for their immunizations, the doctor will hand them a banana. More importantly, perhaps sometime soon, millions of children in poor countries will be saved.

Write your answers.

1. Write two advantages and two drawbacks to Arntzen's plan.

   Advantages: _____

   _____

   Drawbacks: _____

   _____

   _____

2. Did the author offer a balanced or a biased viewpoint of banana vaccinations? Why did you reach this conclusion? _____

   _____

3. Now that you have read the article, have you refined your judgment about the practicality of or need for banana vaccinations? Has the information in the article instead backed up your original judgment? Write your refined judgment about banana vaccinations, including at least two supporting facts from the article.

   _____

   _____

   _____

   _____

Name _____

A Jungle Palace

Articles often include specific details and sensory images. Specific details may tell you the size of an object or the age of a person. Sensory images may tell you how something looks, smells, tastes, sounds, or feels when touched. You can use these details or sensory images to form pictures in your mind. This process is called *visualization*. Read the article about the Maya palace. Circle any specific details or sensory images that help you visualize the palace.

Arthur A. Demarest hunts for archeological treasures. In the remote jungle of Guatemala, he stumbled on the biggest treasure he has ever found: a 170-room Maya palace hidden for centuries.

Demarest, an archeologist, teaches at Vanderbilt University. He also studies Maya civilization. The Maya civilization flowered from A.D. 250 to A.D. 900, and the palace came from that period.

In 1990 Demarest traveled to Cancún to follow up on a lead. While walking on top of a hill in the jungle, he fell into a pit filled with lush, green vegetation. The hill was not a hill. A tangle of palms, vines, and the occasional orchid covered a three-story palace. He had just discovered one of the 11 palace courtyards.

Until that time, most archeologists believed that Maya society was organized around warfare and religion, but the palace included no temples or relics of warfare. Archeologists began questioning their ideas about Maya civilization. With persistence, a knowledgeable guess, and perhaps a little luck, Demarest changed the way modern educators viewed Maya history.

The details or sensory images in this article might have helped you visualize the palace at Cancún. Write an opening paragraph for a travel brochure to Cancún. Invite travelers to visit the palace as it existed during the flowering of the Maya civilization or invite them to visit an archeological dig, seeing the site as it existed when Demarest discovered it.

_____

_____

_____

_____

Name _____

A Letter to Mike

Imagine that you found a letter tucked inside a second-hand book. The paper has yellowed from age. As you read the letter, think about the details you encounter. What conclusions can you draw about the letter writer, the setting, and the person to whom the letter was addressed?

Dear Mike,

Well, I'm 14! My birthday didn't seem right without my older brother, but at least you left me your hi-fi to use while you were gone! Mom and Dad got me a new 45. It's an Elvis Presley song, "Suspicion."

Mom just walked by and told me to write something cheerful, but it's so hard to stay cheerful. In school today, we practiced crouching under our desks with our hands over our heads in case Cuba bombs us. Mom and Dad packed the hall closet with blankets, canned food, and water. Dad thinks it's likely our town would be one of the first targets because of all the refineries here on the Gulf of Mexico. Plus, we're so close to Cuba. Dad showed me how to stuff the blanket around the edges of the door in case I was home alone when a bomb alert sounded. He told me not to open the door to anyone, not even him or Mom, not even if they begged. It makes me cry to think about leaving Dad and Mom outside to die from radiation poisoning.

Dad said we should be proud of you for helping to protect our country, but Mom and I just want you home. Hurry home.

Love,
Brenda

Write your answers.

1. The torn portion of the letter must have included the date. List two ways you might determine the year in which this letter was written.

   _____

   _____

2. Brenda does not mention the name of her town. Name two clues she gives to her town's location.

   _____

   _____

3. Many refinery towns ring the Gulf of Mexico. Is it probable that Brenda lived in one of those towns? ____ With the clues given in the letter, could you look at a map and determine in which of these towns Brenda lived? ____ Why or why not?

   _____

Name _____

Spacewalk Drills

Imagine that you have five minutes before class begins and you have not yet completed your homework. That's okay, because your teacher assigned a crossword puzzle. You will find all the information you need in the article on the next page. First, glance at the puzzle clues, noting which details you will need. Then scan the article, looking for the needed clues.

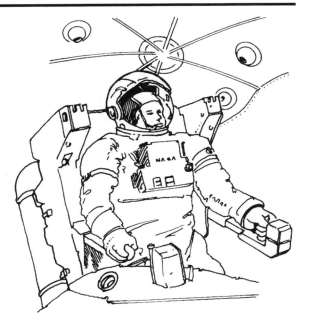

Across

1. number of astronauts working together in a recent spacewalking drill
4. number of spacewalking excursions needed to construct the space station
6. place where future astronauts train

Down

1. number of minutes required to travel 50 feet in a recent spacewalking drill
2. author's suggested new name for jet packs
3. number of feet the jet packs propelled astronauts on a recent spacewalking drill
5. place from which astronauts stepped into space in a recent spacewalking drill

In the deep silence of space, an unconscious astronaut drifts, arms and legs akimbo. You've probably seen this scene in the movies, but as of this writing, it has never occurred on a real space mission. Still, NASA fears that it might some day. Construction of the space station will require at least 165 spacewalking excursions. Maintenance and tests will require more excursions outside the station. More space walks mean more opportunities for mishaps. In the past, the shuttle commander could just drive the shuttle over to pick up a drifting astronaut, but in the future, the shuttle might be docked or might even be back on Earth. The shuttle might be unavailable for rescues.

Whenever time allows, astronauts practice space rescues, just as you might have fire drills at school or home. Mission planners use the test results to create computer simulations back at NASA's virtual-reality lab, where future astronauts train. In one practice session in space, astronauts worked in pairs. They took turns stepping off the shuttle from the tip of the robot arm. To make certain that the astronauts could return in this training session, they were connected to the arm by two braided steel tethers.

Astronauts tend to tumble in space. NASA was not sure that tumbling astronauts could orient themselves and get back to the shuttle. The drills proved that astronauts could easily control the systems meant to keep them from tumbling. Jet packs powered them 50 feet away from the space station and then back again.

Maybe those jet packs should be called "mosey packs" instead. The astronauts did not exactly jet from one spot to another. Astronauts spent about 30 minutes traveling that 50-foot distance away from the shuttle arm and then back again.

Name _____

Vacation by Computer

You have planned your entire spring break when your mother cancels the family's plans. She has got a big new project and has to travel, but you and your brother are going along. You have only five days to make new plans. Below you will find a listing of the information you call up when you do an Internet city search. Look at the information available on this page, then answer the questions below.

1. You will be in town the third through the seventh of the month. To find out what's happening on those days, you click on _____.

2. You are interested in basketball. The city you are visiting does not have a professional team, but maybe they have a good college team. Where do you go to find out?

   _____

3. Your mother has promised to take you to see the latest movie on the fourth, after she finishes her workday, but only if she can find a sitter for your four-year-old brother. To find a hotel that offers baby-sitting services, you start by searching _____.

4. Now it is time to look up local movie theaters. The first place you check would probably be _____.

5. You have found several theaters showing the movie you want. How do you find out which one is closest to the hotel? _____

Name _____

Mapping It Out

Over the winter vacation, you are planning a trip to sunny Texas to visit friends. Your plane lands at Dallas-Ft. Worth Airport, where your parents rent a car and head out for Breckenridge, the place where your former neighbors moved when they came to Texas. But much to your dismay, as you start your journey on Route 180 near Mineral Wells, you find out on the radio that Route 180 (the road you're on) has just been closed at Mineral Wells because of icy road conditions. So you start to retrace your path to try another route. On further check with the Texas Highway Department, you find the following roads are also closed:

180 west of Mineral Wells to Caddo
Rt. 6 north of Dublin
207 north of Ranger
183 north of I-20

Write your answers:
1. Will you be able to travel from Dallas-Ft. Worth to your friends in Breckenridge?____

2. Write down the route you and your family must take from the western edge of Ft. Worth to Breckenridge. _____

_____

_____

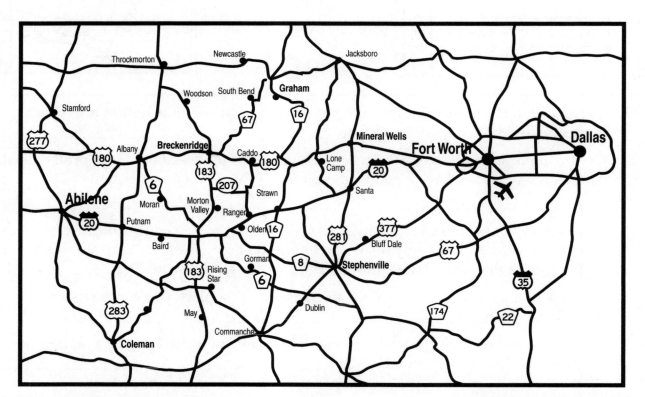

Supplying Electricity

Authors use details to build upon main ideas, just as masons use bricks to build walls. Each detail should fit that main idea, just as each brick should fit smoothly into a wall. As you read this selection, think about the details you notice. How do they fit together? What main idea do they build?

Deep in the rainforests of Guatemala, night falls on a darkened village. A teen struggles to do schoolwork by firelight but gives up and puts the book away. No electrical lines run to this small village.

Photovoltaic or solar cells can provide electricity to small villages in third-world countries. Solar cells change the sun's energy into usable electricity. Solar energy can power radios and fans in out-of-the-way villages. It recharges batteries. It powers sun ovens.

Once, scientists predicted that most of us would live in solar-powered homes by the turn of the twenty-first century. These scientists believed that solar energy would run watches, cars, satellites, and even such luxuries as machines that froth milk for cappuccino. They noted that solar energy produces less pollution. Solar-powered appliances cost less to run. These scientists' predictions fell short. Solar-powered homes cost more to build. In areas with ready access to electricity, few people wanted to spend the extra money.

The cost considerations change for isolated villages. Electrical lines must be extended across difficult and sometimes dangerous terrain. The costs prove enormous and few developing countries can afford to pay those costs. Solar cells cost less than paying for the electrical lines. Perhaps that explains why 70 percent of the world's photovoltaic cells now go to third-world countries.

Write your answers.

1. Write four details from the fourth paragraph of "Supplying Electricity."

   _____

   _____

   _____

   _____

2. Below are two graphic representations of main ideas. Most details from this selection would help build either of these main ideas, but the details from the fourth paragraph would fit only one of these main ideas. The details in that paragraph would be off the point for the other suggested main idea.

   Study the main ideas that top the two walls. Which wall (A or B) would the details from the fourth paragraph help build?_____

A.

Solar cells prove more beneficial to third-world countries than to developed countries.

Solar cells power radios and fans.

Electrical lines cannot be run to some villages.

Solar cells change the sun's energy into usable electricity.

Solar cells cost less than extending electrical lines.

B.

Solar energy benefits third-world villages.

Solar cells power radios and fans.

Electrical lines cannot be run to some villages.

Solar cells change the sun's energy into usable electricity.

Solar cells cost less than extending electrical lines.

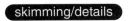

Name _____

The Irish Famine

Imagine that you have an essay test today on the Irish famine. Your teacher lets you bring notes to class, but they must fit on a 3" x 5" card. Skim this article, getting a sense of its main idea. Put a check mark beside any detail that might help you discuss the effects of the Irish famine, but do not slow your reading to write down that detail.

On May 1, 1848, the *Swan* set sail from Cork, Ireland. The ship carried victims of the Irish famine toward a new life in America.

Behind them, the passengers left fields black with rot and relatives dying of starvation and disease. Ahead stretched a dangerous voyage. On ships transporting victims of the famine, cholera sometimes passed from one passenger to the next, infecting everyone and killing up to one-third of the passengers.

A single crop started the trouble. Through the generations, Irish parents and their grown children divided farms into smaller and smaller lots. Because potatoes could be grown on the small lots, poor Irish families eventually depended almost entirely on this plant for food. Most families grew the same varieties of potatoes. When blight was accidentally introduced into the country in 1845, all those varieties would prove susceptible. Year after year, the crops died. So did the Irish people. So many people died that relatives could not obtain coffins. The famine would be the worst European famine in all of the 1800s.

The famine changed Ireland forever. Afterward, farmers tried new methods and new crops. They varied their diets. They mourned the people they had lost through death or immigration to North America and Britain. In 1844 Ireland's population was about 8,400,000. By 1851 more than one million would be dead, and a million and a half would have emigrated to North America and Britain, many on ships like the *Swan*. The lowly potato had changed a country and a people forever.

Now use the space at the right to jot down the specific details you checked. Choose the ones that might be most important if you were to write an essay on the Irish famine.

High-Tech Plastic Swimming Pools

This article tells how researchers used a surprising tool to find treasures hidden beneath the soil. That is the main idea, but not the theme. The theme would be an idea about life, formed after reading the article.

A theme might be something broad, such as the idea that rumors spread fast. Sometimes proverbs can be good at expressing themes. For example, a Chinese proverb says that a rumor goes in one ear and out many mouths.

Below you will find four proverbs from four different cultures, found on *Brain Candy's* Web site. Read the proverbs first. Then read "High-Tech Plastic Swimming Pools," noticing the theme the author develops. Then put a check beside the proverb that best relates to that theme.

_____ 1. Feather by feather the goose can be plucked: a French proverb.

_____ 2. He who would climb a ladder must start at the bottom: an English proverb.

_____ 3. If you believe everything you read, better not read: a Japanese proverb.

_____ 4. Necessity is the mother of invention: an Irish proverb.

Researchers at the University of Illinois at Urbana-Champaign use high-tech tools. They use children's plastic swimming pools.

In reports in the *Journal of the Acoustical Society of America* and university newsletters, Professor William O'Brien, Jr., describes the events that led to the swimming-pool episode. All across America and other countries, archeological treasure might be hidden beneath the soil, O'Brien says. New building construction could damage those treasures. Radar cannot detect pottery, skeletons, or other nonmetallic objects. Sometimes builders must sift through the dirt before digging foundations, but the process proves expensive.

O'Brien's team decided to use ultrasound to locate buried objects. Ultrasound bounces sound off objects, and computers form an image of the object hit by the sound waves.

The researchers ran into a problem. They needed a way to spread the sound waves across a wider area. A thin layer of water would spread them, but wetting the soil would not work. Sound waves would not penetrate as far into wet soil. A child's swimming pool might work, the researchers decided. The pool would hold a thin layer of water, allowing the researchers to spread the sound waves across a bigger area of soil. The plan worked. In tests at the university, researchers located several objects, including a glass bottle.

O'Brien and his team proved that ultrasound could be used to locate nonmetallic objects beneath the soil. They will eventually need something more high-tech than a child's swimming pool, but for now, their research has made a splash with both builders and archeologists.

Golden Words

During the Civil War, Americans took sides against each other. Each side was biased against the other's views. Authors can be biased, too. Material may appear to be factual, but a careful examination can show that the author does not present all viewpoints. Sometimes loaded words also show the author's bias. Other times, the author might use more subtle tools such as irony or satire to present a biased viewpoint. Irony occurs when the outcome of an event differs from the expected outcome. Read this profile of a Confederate spy, watching for any loaded words or ironic situations that might betray a bias on the part of the author.

Rose O'Neal Greenhow sighed. She picked up the pen and leaned forward, writing the secretary of state's address at the top of a sheet of stationery. She had just begun the letter that she hoped would result in her freedom.

She protested that she had been unfairly imprisoned. Jailers held her and her daughter in Washington's Old Capitol Prison. "And thus for a period of seven days, I, with my little child, was placed absolutely at the mercy of men without character or responsibility," Greenhow wrote in the 1861 letter, now in a collection at Duke University.

People usually paid attention to Greenhow. Nick-named "Wild Rose" when still a child, she grew up to be a famous hostess. As the Civil War loomed, she spoke often and passionately about her views. She opposed Lincoln's decisions.

When the war broke, Greenhow did not stop talking. She just did it in secret. She worked secretly by becoming a Confederate spy. So important was the information she leaked that some credit her with helping the Confederates win two important battles. She managed to get information to the Confederates even after her imprisonment, hiding messages in women visitors' hair and other unlikely places.

Greenhow's letter did not win her immediate release, but she was eventually released. She was exiled to the Confederacy. From there she traveled to England, where she used her skill with words to drum up sympathy for Confederate causes. She also wrote her prison memoirs, and her publishers paid her in gold.

Those golden words proved to be her undoing. When she was returning from England on the *Condor,* a Union gunboat pursued the vessel. The *Condor* ran aground. Greenhow escaped in a rowboat, but that boat capsized, too. The weight of the gold dragged Greenhow down. She drowned, killed by the weight of her own words.

Write your answers.

1. The author could have written the article without including Greenhow's nickname as a child. Why do you think the author included this detail? What image do you think the author wanted to create in your mind?

   _____

2. The author could have written about Greenhow's death without telling that it was the weight of the gold that drowned her. Why do you think the author included this detail?

   _____

   _____

3. In your opinion, did the writer want you to admire Greenhow's courage and defiance or to feel that Greenhow's impulsiveness and defiance led to her own death? Support your opinion with an example from the profile.

   _____

   _____

   _____

   _____

   _____

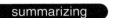

Name _____

An fMRI for Your Thoughts

"I can't understand this," your friend complains, handing you a copy of an article. Read the article so that you can explain the material to your friend. Take your time, rereading difficult passages so that you are certain that you understand them.

Doctors can read your thoughts. At least they can if you consent to an fMRI test.

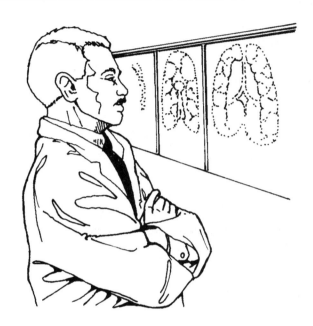

fMRI stands for functional magnetic resonance imaging. In regular magnetic resonance imaging, MRI, a machine bounces sound waves off organs and bones. A computer then studies the pattern of the bounced sound waves. The computer uses this pattern to produce images of the organs and bones. Functional magnetic resonance imaging goes further. It studies the body while the body functions or works. It can see blood flowing. More blood flows to active parts of the brain, so some doctors study the thinking brain using an fMRI.

Perhaps researchers cannot yet identify exactly what you might be thinking, but they are close. Studying the fMRIs of volunteers, doctors learned to identify which parts of the brain showed activity when volunteers felt frightened or amused. They determined when volunteers detected a certain odor or felt other sensations. They noticed which part of the brain received more blood flow when volunteers listened to a joke.

Why would researchers care what you are thinking? People who have suffered brain injuries may have difficulty with moving, remembering, speaking, or even feeling emotions. If scientists can identify how the brain works, perhaps they can retrain injured brains to think.

Now paraphrase the material, telling your friend why it is important to know about fMRIs and how they can be used. Remember that when you paraphrase, you summarize the author's ideas, not your own.

_____

_____

_____

_____

Name _____

Secret Pal

You've had a bad week, and someone noticed. Every day when you sign on to your family's computer, you find an e-mailed card. You've received a "Thinking of You" card, a "Weary Willie Day" card, and a "Night of the Lizard King" card. The sender used your family's screen name but signed the card "Someone Who Cares."

To find out which family member sent the cards, you check the Internet history screen, which tracks the sites that have been visited. The most recent sites are listed first. To study the sites in the order in which they were visited, begin at the bottom of the list and work your way up. As you examine the history, you remind yourself that your architect mother invests in the stock market. She is looking for a new job and is considering moving the family to a new city. Your father loves mountain biking and checking his investments on Marketwatch. You remember him telling your brother that he had found a cool site for mountain-biking vacations. Your brother said he would check the site, too, as soon as he finished checking the Rockets' homepage, to see when the next home game would be. Remembering these facts will help you decipher the list and figure out the identity of your secret pal. Who probably sent the cards? _____

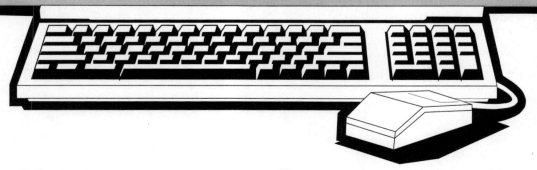

Success!
PREVIEW—Night of the Lizard King
Night of the Lizard King
Wacky Holiday eCards from Blue Mountain
Blue Mountain—The World's Favorite eCards
iExplore/Trip Search/Results
The Official Site of the Houston Rockets
Success!
PREVIEW—Weary Willie Day
Weary Willie Day
iExplore/Trip Details
iExplore/Trip Search/Results
mountainbiking.com
CBS.Marketwatch.com—The Story Behind the
Numbers

Success!
PREVIEW—a little note
A little note
Thinking of You eCards from Blue Mountain
Camelback Mountain—Phoenix
Phoenix: Search Results—City Search
City Search: Phoenix: city & visitor's guide
City Search: Phoenix
citysearch.com
US—AZ—Phoenix—Job Captain/Architect
Jobs—Monster.com

IF87029 *Nonfiction Reading Comprehension*

Mummies Have No Secrets

Anthropologists use an important tool: classifying (or categorizing). Readers can use this tool, too. As you read this article about mummies, think about the ways you might classify or categorize the information you learn.

Mummies cannot hide their age. They cannot hide what they ate for their last meals or whether their families were wealthy or poor. Mummies cannot hide much of anything from anthropologists.

Wrappings and artifacts reveal much about the social status of the person while alive. For example, a mummy found in the Taklimakan Desert sported a bronze earring and leather boots. The decorations on these items showed that his people were skilled artisans.

A mummy's body reveals even more clues than its wrappings. The contents of a mummy's digestive tract can be examined chemically and microscopically, giving anthropologists clues about the person's diet. When anthropologists studied the Iceman, a mummy found in Italy, they examined the contents of his intestines. They wanted to see what he ate in the hours before his death. Organs and bones reveal details about the way the person died, too. Even if no flesh remains, bones and teeth might reveal the age of the person at death, as well as some details about diet, height, occupation, ethnicity, and social status. A male mummy's worn front teeth might indicate that he used his teeth to hold a tool, freeing his hands for other work. In addition, since bone absorbs minerals during a person's life, a chemical study of the bones turns up information about the diet of the deceased person. If DNA can be extracted from a mummy, scientists can even determine the blood type of the deceased person.

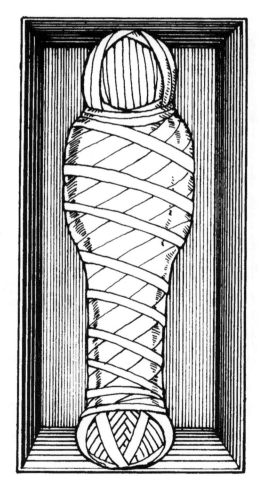

Even death and 5,000 years cannot hide a mummy's secrets. These secrets are contributing to what we know about ancient life.

1. Imagine that you are part of a team of anthropologists who discovers several mummies in a mountainous setting. The mummies appear to include people of several different ages and to come from many different social groups. Some are skeletal and some almost lifelike. Your team divides into two groups to study the mummies. Each group will determine different information about these mummies. They also will study different items. If one group examines an item, the other group will not also examine that item. That makes their tasks mutually exclusive. The responsibilities of each team have been listed below. Study the listed responsibilities, then write mutually exclusive titles for each group.

   Title 1 _____   Title 2 _____
   This group will determine   This group will determine the following:
   the following: social status
   age of a person at death   food eaten at last meal
   height

2. Imagine that you are part of a team of anthropologists who discovers a desert burial site. You unearth a number of mummies. A quick examination shows that they were buried at the site across a span of three centuries, they were both male and female, and they were of all ages and all social groups. Name four ways you could categorize the mummies.

   _____
   _____
   _____
   _____

Welcome to Life as a Cyborg!

Sometimes an author uses loaded words that reveal bias. Sometimes an author uses more subtle methods to communicate a bias. For example, an author might use exaggerations or deliberate understatements. An author might pretend to admire a development or an idea, while actually mocking it. An author who employs these more subtle tactics is using satire. Read the following article, looking for the different methods the author uses to reveal bias.

Kevin Warwick might call himself a cyborg.

Science-fiction fans define *cyborgs* as "blends of human and machine." Warwick directed doctors to implant silicon chips under his skin, making him a blend of human and machine. One chip tracks his position. It can open doors for him, turn on lights, and perform other interesting and helpful functions. He hopes the next one will monitor the electrical signals his brain sends through his body. His wife wants a chip, too. Warwick believes that it is possible that he can make his wife's hand move if he moves his own hand.

Some people might see a few problems with this whole setup, but Warwick remains enthusiastic. So do the companies developing chips. Companies plan that their chips can track the elderly and listen to their heartbeats and breathing, monitor travelers' or prisoners' positions anywhere on the globe, and track children as they make their way home from school.

If Warwick proves right, not only can your parents follow your every move, but they also can make certain that you practice your music lesson. They can manipulate your hands and fingers if you do not feel inclined to practice on your own.

It gets weirder. Warwick thinks that people can share emotions with each other, through their silicon chips. While your parents observe your location and enforce your practice schedule, they can also monitor whether you are feeling a little out of sorts about the whole thing.

If you are a little worried at the thought of your parents controlling so much of your life, Warwick has an answer for that, too. On a good day, you can record your happy emotions on your chip, and then play those emotions back on an out-of-sorts day. Your parents need never know that you are unhappy. In fact, maybe you will never feel unhappy again.

Name _____

Write your answers.

1. Write an example of a loaded word or phrase that the author used.

   _____

2. The author proposes that your parents might be able to manipulate your hands if you do not feel inclined to practice on your own. In your opinion, does the author intend this to be an accurate statement of the possibilities of implanted silicon chips, an exaggeration, or a deliberate understatement?

   _____

3. The third paragraph begins with a statement that some people might see a few problems. Would you guess that this an accurate statement of the author's actual belief, an exaggeration, or a deliberate understatement?

   _____

4. This author called some functions of implanted chips interesting and helpful. This is an example of _____.

5. What would you guess the author wants you to believe about implanting silicon chips into humans?

   _____

6. Write another paragraph that seems to praise some imagined benefit of implanting silicon chips into humans, using loaded words, satire, exaggeration, or deliberate understatement.

   _____

   _____

   _____

   _____

   _____

   _____

   _____

   _____

   _____

Name _____

Virus Killers

Articles sometimes discuss scientific developments. These scientific articles may contain up-to-date information about research in medicine, astronomy, physics, and other areas of science. They often include both facts and theories. Researchers propose theories—their best opinions about how the facts can be interpreted. Facts can be proven true or false. Theories can be tested and shown to hold true or to fail, but they cannot be proven true or false. When you read the following article about virus killers, think about which statements are factual and which discuss the opinions of the researchers.

Got a cold? Somewhere, a scientist may be designing a custom cure.

In the past, researchers found cures by a trial-and-error process. They screened all kinds of compounds to see which worked on which kind of illness. Sometimes, no compound seemed to work. For example, doctors could give medications that eased the symptoms of a cold, but they could not cure colds.

Viruses cause colds. They cause more serious diseases, too, such as meningitis, an inflammation of the brain. Doctors had few medications to use against viruses since antibiotics do not help with viral illness. Antibiotics kill bacteria but do not affect viruses.

Now new tools, such as the electron microscope, allow scientists to look at cold viruses and see their structures. Researchers hope to design a cure that locks into grooves in the virus. With the grooves already filled, the virus cannot link with other structures it needs to survive. It dies. The cold goes away.

At least, that is what scientists hope will happen. They are still hard at work, custom designing the perfect cure for the common cold.

Write F for fact or O for opinion.

_____ 1. Viruses cause colds.

_____ 2. Antibiotics do not cure viral illnesses.

_____ 3. Scientists can custom-design cures that lock into the grooves in viruses.

_____ 4. The electron microscope allows scientists to look at viruses and see their structures.

_____ 5. In the past, researchers found cures by a trial-and-error process.

_____ 6. Antibiotics work against bacterial illnesses by killing the bacteria.

Name _____

The Old Days Weren't Like You Thought

Generalizations are statements that predict something about a whole group of people or things. *Cats don't like water* is a generalization about cats. Authors sometimes make generalizations, and so do other people. Some generalizations are valid, but some prove to be faulty. The reading selection on this page discusses Ice Age people and the way they dressed and lived. Before you read this selection, write down four generalizations you might make about prehistoric people.

_____

_____

_____

_____

Now read the article. As you read, reexamine and refine your ideas about prehistoric people.

If you traveled back in time to the Ice Age, you would want to take Olga Soffer with you. She could tell you what to wear.

You'd wear furs and animal skins, stitched together with sinew, right? Not necessarily, Soffer would say. A former immigrant from Yugoslavia, Soffer focused her archeological research on Eastern Europe. While she and an associate were studying pottery statues found there, they discovered evidence that well-dressed prehistoric people might have worn clothes much like our fine cottons and linens.

Fine marks crisscrossed the pottery. Soffer examined those marks. Before studying prehistoric art and life, she had worked for ten years in the fashion industry. She recognized those marks as evidence of woven threads. Soffer and her colleague decided that the statues had once been dressed in woven clothing. Through the ages, the clothing had disintegrated, leaving the marks as the only evidence of its existence.

Women would have woven that clothing. Until recently, anthropologists focused on the man in prehistoric societies. Their stone tools sometimes survived the passage of time. The plant fibers that women wove into clothing did not survive. Soffer's research forced anthropologists to rethink women's contributions to their prehistoric society.

Were any of your generalizations faulty? If so, rewrite the generalization, incorporating the new ideas you gleaned from the reading selection.

_____

_____

_____

_____

What's This?

Mount Saint Helens erupted in May 1980, killing 57 people. The eruption covered mountainsides and homes with ash and magma. Imagine that you are an archeologist from the twenty-fifth century, working to uncover one of those homes. You discover something puzzling that does not seem to belong to American life in the twentieth century.

Study the drawing. Notice what you see in the drawing. Think who might have used these items and what their purpose might have been.

What kind of items are these? Write your first conclusion. You will refine this conclusion as you examine the item and discover new clues.

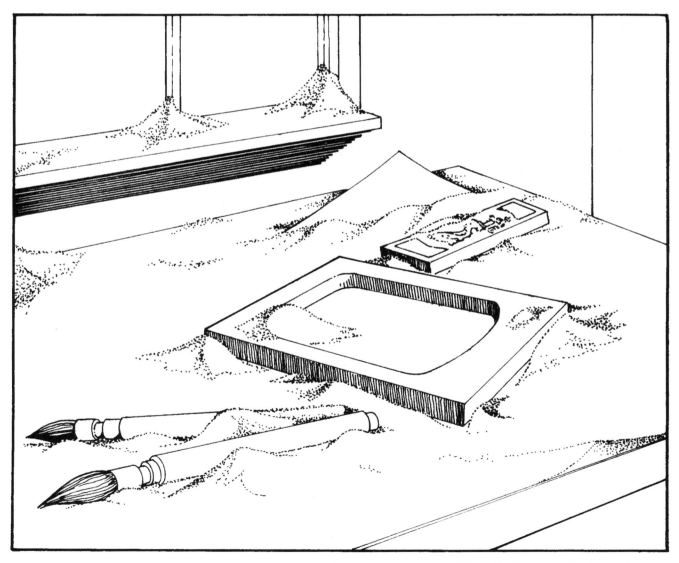

Now study the new clues listed below.

1. Clue one: Someone formed one of the objects out of a gum-like substance and soot. Refine your original conclusion.

   _____

   _____

2. Clue two: Someone shaped stone or pottery to make one of the objects. Refine your conclusion.

   _____

   _____

3. Clue three: The decorations on one of the objects is Chinese. Refine your conclusion.

   _____

   _____

4. Clue four: People used these tools throughout China's history and into modern times. Refine your conclusion.

   _____

   _____

5. Clue five: These tools form something that has been compared to dance, animal tracks, or abstract art. Refine your conclusion.

   _____

   _____

6. Clue six: To use these tools, water was put on the flat stone. Refine your conclusion.

   _____

   _____

7. Clue seven: Paper and brushes are often used together with these two tools. Refine your conclusion.

   _____

   _____

8. Now look back at your first conclusion. Was it accurate? If not, what might have led to this first inaccurate conclusion?

   _____

   _____

Name _____

Al Capp and an American Tradition

As you read this article about Al Capp and the tradition he began, notice details that might support the main idea.

Does your school have a Sadie Hawkins' dance? Girls ask boys to Sadie Hawkins' events. The first Sadie Hawkins' dance took place in November 1938.

Alfred Gerald Caplin, later known as Al Capp, started the tradition. When nine-year-old Alfred first began to sketch, he probably was not planning to create an enduring American folk event. He wanted something to fire his imagination and give him hope. Caplin had just lost his left leg in a trolley accident, and his father had encouraged him to draw cartoons during his recovery.

As an adult, Caplin wrote cartoons under the name Al Capp. In 1934 he began a strip called "Li'l Abner." Capp's cartoon featured out-of-luck people. The characters appealed to Americans living through the Great Depression, and Capp soon became known for a mocking humorous style that helped Americans rethink their way of life.

In the late 1930s, women did not often chase men, but Capp's Sadie Hawkins did. In a cartoon published on November 15, 1937, Sadie and her friends chased the men of Dogpatch, looking for likely husbands. Sadie's daring act caught the attention of people across America. The first official Sadie Hawkins' Day events occurred a year later, in 1938. By 1939 more than 200 schools and colleges held Sadie Hawkins' Day events. Dances were often a part of these celebrations. A national institution had been born of a boy's attempts to create a new life.

Some details are more important than others. Read each pair of statements below. Decide which statement includes the details that most help readers understand how or why Al Capp created a new American tradition. Put a check beside that statement.

_____ 1. Caplin lost his left leg in a trolley accident.

_____   Caplin began to draw cartoons after losing his leg in a trolley accident.

_____ 2. Al Capp's characters lived in a town called Dogpatch.

_____   In Al Capp's cartoon, a character called Sadie Hawkins chased the men, looking for a likely husband.

_____ 3. "Li'l Abner" was introduced in 1934.

_____   "Li'l Abner" was introduced during the Depression, when Americans needed a reason to laugh.

_____ 4. In the late 1930s, women did not often chase men.

_____   Alfred Caplin wrote under the name Al Capp.

Name _____

Bacteria Eat Toxic Waste

This article includes words printed in bold type. These words have more than one meaning. Read the article, thinking about how the words in bold type are used in the context.

What do you get if you mix common bacteria and vinegar?

This is not the beginning of a **lame** joke. It is a serious science question. You get bacteria that eat toxic **waste** and turn that waste into salt.

Bacteria can make you sick, but not all **strains** of bacteria are harmful. Some bacteria benefit humans. Now scientists propose a new, beneficial use for bacteria: bioremediation. Bioremediation uses specialized microorganisms for toxic cleanup. Vinegar stimulates these bacteria to consume the toxic liquids. The bacteria transform the toxins into salt. The bacteria function in closed-in places, without sunlight, and they produce oxygen as a by-product. Some scientists wonder if they could be put to use in mines or during prolonged space travel, where they could digest waste products and produce needed oxygen.

Other scientists wonder whether bacteria could digest radioactive wastes, too. Scientists **introduced** one type of bacteria into water that contained dissolved uranium. The bacteria went to work, transforming the uranium-laden water into water mixed with a harmless solid. Geneticists propose customizing bacteria to work on specific types of wastes, including nuclear waste. Already, geneticists have inserted genes from one bacteria into another type of bacteria, creating a superbug. Laboratory tests show that the superbug transformed toxic mercury in nuclear waste to less toxic forms.

Customized bacteria. What will science think of next?

Circle the correct answer.

1. As used in the article, **lame** means
   a. having a stiff or sore arm or leg.
   b. a thin metal plate.
   c. disabled.
   d. weak.

2. As used in the article, **waste** means
   a. misuse.
   b. litter.
   c. unwanted refuse or by-products.
   d. leftovers.

3. As used in the article, **strains** means
   a. types.
   b. injuries.
   c. twists.
   d. pulls.

4. As used in the article, **introduced** means
   a. begun.
   b. presented.
   c. added.
   d. started.

Curious Animals

Concept or word maps are great tools. They help you visualize the material and see how the details relate to one another. Concept maps start with a single word or phrase that tells the main topic. Try making a concept map for "Curious Animals," the article on this page.

On the following page, you will find the topic of "Curious Animals" enclosed in an oval. As you skim the article, getting a sense of what is being discussed, also look for important words or concepts. Jot them down on the concept map. Draw lines that connect related ideas.

Curiosity killed the cat. Many of us have heard this saying, most often when someone wants to avoid answering our questions. A more accurate saying might be that curiosity taught the cat.

Animals exhibit many kinds of learning. Russian scientist Ivan Pavlov always rang a bell before feeding a group of dogs. His research showed that the dogs soon began salivating whenever they heard the bell. He had conditioned them to expect food. Conditioning is one type of learning. Other types include trial and error, latent learning, imprinting, insight, and play or curiosity.

Both adults and young animals might play, but young animals play more often. Curiosity seems linked to play behaviors. Curious animals play more. They explore. They develop new motor skills. A curious lion cub may bat at a creeping insect, developing the coordination she will need to catch prey. Curious animals see, hear, smell, touch, and taste new things. They learn.

Not all animals exhibit play behaviors. Mammals and birds may play, but fish, invertebrates, and amphibians have not been observed playing. Play behavior requires initiative and a willingness to seek new experiences.

Initiative and openness to new experiences are good traits, aren't they?

To test your note-taking ability, answer the following questions without referring back to "Curious Animals." Use the information from your concept map.

1. How does curiosity or play help animals to learn?

   _____

   _____

   _____

2. What type of learning did Pavlov's experiments explore?

   _____

3. Name three types of learning.

   _____

   _____

   _____

4. Do young toads seem to play?

   _____

Curious Animals

Name _____

Infections in Space

Scientists draw conclusions from the observations they make. As you read, you also draw conclusions. Authors often provide the information you need to draw conclusions. After studying the information the author provides, you can predict that something might happen, even if you have never had experience with the situation the author describes. As you read this article about infections in space, think about the conclusions you can draw.

If you do not like housecleaning, do not apply to the astronaut program. Astronauts clean. Their lives depend on it.

Astronauts carry microorganisms into space with them. That is inevitable, since all people harbor microorganisms. Most remain harmless, but in space, radiation can cause microorganisms to mutate. The new forms might be harmful. Astronauts would not have any natural immunity to these mutated forms since they would never have been exposed to the new forms. Also, studies show that immunity lessens in space, making astronauts even more susceptible to these mutated microorganisms.

Astronauts observed mold and mildew on the windows and equipment of the Mir space station. That reinforced the idea that microorganisms can take hold and grow in space. Astronauts also reported strange smells. This evidence of growing microorganisms in space makes scientists worry about what will happen when humans spend longer times in a spacecraft. Scientists estimate that travel to Mars will require astronauts to spend two years in their spacecraft, plenty of time for microorganisms to multiply. In addition, this voyage would expose the craft to even more radiation, perhaps producing even more mutations.

What's the answer? Newly developed filters grab microorganisms right out of the air. Also, a new formulation of a household toilet-cleaning tablet helps astronauts keep their toilets clean. Sometimes, though, the solution proves distinctively less high tech. Astronauts still clean house.

Write your answers.
1. What conclusion could you draw about the length of time the space station Mir was used? _____

2. What relationship exists between the length of space travel and the growth of microorganisms inside a spacecraft? Think about the conclusion you can draw after reading this article. _____
   _____

3. How useful do you think known medications would be against the mutated microorganisms astronauts might encounter in space? _____
   _____

Name _____

Previewing the Past

Sometimes illustrations reveal important details. Those details might relate to the main topic of articles. Imagine that the illustration on this page tops a magazine page, and that an article follows. Preview this illustration of men delivering a block of ice, noticing the details. Then answer the questions below the illustration.

Fill in the blank with the letter of the best answer.

_____ 1. This drawing probably pictures a time when . . .
   a. a family took a holiday in the country.
   b. most families did not have electric refrigerators and needed to have ice delivered.

_____ 2. This drawing probably pictures a _____ day.
   a. warm
   b. cold

_____ 3. The men in this illustration probably . . .
   a. intend to deliver the ice to the home pictured in the background.
   b. just cut the ice from a pond.

_____ 4. The men in the illustration probably . . .
   a. arrived at this location in the vehicle that is visible in the illustration.
   b. walked to this location.

_____ 5. What kind of article would include this illustration? The sentences below give suggestions for the main idea. Choose the one that best fits this illustration.
   a. The Civil War period was a time of deprivation in the Deep South.
   b. Life without electricity presented special challenges.
   c. Cars used to be bigger than they are now.
   d. Houses used to be smaller than they are now.

Rabid Vampires

Read this article, thinking about the comparisons the author makes. Then answer the questions that follow.

He wandered the dark night. During the day, he shrank from strong light. He avoided mirrors. He bared his teeth when he smelled garlic. When he died, horrified seventh-century villagers reported that his body still looked lifelike.

Was he one of the undead, a vampire? More likely, he was a victim of rabies, reports Spanish neurologist Juan Gomez-Alonso. The symptoms of rabies victims bear a remarkable similarity to those of so-called vampires, the neurologist thinks.

Legends about vampires spread in the late 1600s. Since then, books and movies have prolonged the myths, including the myths about mirrors and garlic. Movies and books claim that vampires drink blood. They portray most vampires as male. They describe them as the undead, as proven by their pale skin and staring eyes. These vampires sleep during the day and wander during the night. Their features change. When they die, their bodies stay lifelike.

Gomez-Alonso noticed that the vampire myths circulated in Poland and Russia at about the same time that rabies swept through these areas. Another rabies epidemic hit Hungary around 1721–1728, at about the same time that many of the myths about vampires flourished. Gomez-Alonso noticed that seven times more men than women contract rabies. He also noted that symptoms of rabies include irritability and sometimes a tendency to bite or attack other humans. About 25% of men infected with rabies bite others, Gomez-Alonso reports. Facial contortions or spasms sometimes change the features of sufferers. Strong light and mirrors or strong odors can trigger these facial spasms and other symptoms of rabies. Gomez-Alonso also stated that sleeplessness and restlessness cause many rabies sufferers to wander at night. Throat muscles spasm, causing rabid people to make hoarse sounds, bare their teeth, or froth at the mouth. Sometimes the froth is bloody. A person who dies of rabies may look almost lifelike because the illness makes blood stay liquid longer. The blood remains visible under the skin even after death, keeping the skin pink and lifelike.

Gomez-Alonso concluded that these similarities between rabies sufferers and vampires proved too strong to ignore. He thinks that the legendary vampires had actually contracted rabies.

Rabies	Vampires

1. Fill out the comparison chart, writing five similarities in the symptoms suffered by people with rabies and the myths associated with vampires.

2. Keeping in mind the comparisons you have just made between rabies symptoms and vampire myths, do you consider Gomez-Alonso's theory reasonable? _____ Why or why not? _____

_____

Name _____

Jimmy's Vow

This page contains the opening and concluding paragraphs of a profile of Jimmy Carter, the thirty-ninth president of the United States. It does not include the middle or body of the article. The middles of most articles provide facts and details that support the main idea. Read the title of the page, as well as the opening and concluding paragraphs. Think about the main idea. What kinds of details or facts would support that main idea?

Opening:

In a sandy cotton field in Georgia, a boy straightened. He held his bleeding hands in front of him. The cotton bolls had sliced his hands, but he wasn't thinking about the cuts. He was imagining different landscapes, like the ones his uncle had seen during his travels in the Navy. The boy promised himself that one day he would enlist in the Navy. He vowed that he would go to college, too, even though none of his family had ever attended college. That boy was James E. Carter, better known as Jimmy, and he would grow up to become president of the United States.

Conclusion:

That boy achieved all he had set out to achieve, plus much he could not have imagined for himself. Through it all, he never forgot what it was like to live among desperately poor people. Instead of isolating himself from the poverty that had surrounded him as a child, he attacked the causes of poverty. Perhaps the example he provides is his greatest accomplishment.

Below are several sentences. Check the ones that might support the main idea of this article.

_____ 1. Cotton plants are relatives of hibiscus, okra, and swamp mallow plants.

_____ 2. After his presidency was over, President Carter volunteered for Habitat for Humanity.

_____ 3. Carter did go to the U.S. Naval Academy, where he studied nuclear physics.

_____ 4. Cotton plants need irrigation.

_____ 5. George Bancroft founded the Naval School, later to become the U.S. Naval Academy, in 1845.

Name _____

Short and Snappy

Imagine that your school needs a catchy, easy-to-remember slogan that will appear on all school-related materials. Each student will submit a suggestion. Before writing your submission, you study popular advertising slogans from the past. You notice that companies often choose short slogans. Some companies choose humorous slogans or slogans that masquerade as commands. Slogans sometimes have mass appeal and sometimes have snob appeal. Some slogans rely on sentiment to make a point. Many slogans employ a rhythmic meter, rhyme or alliteration, or repetition, making them easier to remember. Some slogans use several tactics. Look at the following products and see if you can think of a slogan to advertise each. Then write down the tactic used in the slogan.

Product	Slogan/Tactics
1. Headache medicine	
2. Telephone Company	
3. Soup	
4. Automobile	
5. Margarine	
6. Fast Food	
7. Soda Pop	
8. Detergent	

Using your current school's name, write a slogan advertising the school. Use at least one of the tactics you noticed in the advertising slogans on this page. Identify the tactic or tactics you used.

Slogan: _____

Tactic: _____

Candlestick Charts

Have you ever explained to your parents how to program the VCR? If so, you have been explaining the steps in a process. Taping a program, inserting film into a camera, and downloading information from the Internet all require you to follow certain steps in a process. This article discusses how candlestick charts can be used to predict prices. As you read the portion of the selection that discusses how candlestick charts are drawn, visualize the steps in the process. Then answer the questions that follow on the next page.

Your favorite singing group just broke up, and you have a stash of their CDs, in their original cases. Here is your chance to finance that skiing group you want to attend with classmates. Your CDs may become collector's items. Should you sell them now or hold out for a while longer, hoping that prices will go up?

Candlestick charts might help you predict how the prices will behave. Some people credit Homma, an eighteenth-century Japanese man, with creating candlestick charts. Today, stock traders in the United States and other western countries are rediscovering this ancient form of charting. You can use them, too.

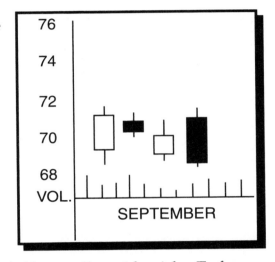

Candlestick charts are a type of bar chart. The bars look like candles with wicks. To form each day's candle, you need four prices: the first price paid for the item that day, the last price, the highest price, and the lowest price. The body of the candle stretches from the first price of the day to the last price of the day. The wick stretches from the highest price of the day to the lowest price of the day. The candles can have both top and bottom wicks or shadows. When prices rise during the day, the last price moves higher than the first price, and the candle is drawn in white. Wicks do not continue through the middle of white candles. When prices fall during the day, the last price moves lower than the first price, and the candle is colored red or black.

If you are selling an item, you want to see lots of white candles on the chart. A white candle signals that buyers paid higher and higher prices throughout that day. Prices might be likely to continue to go up the next day, too. A black or red candle signals that buyers did not show much interest and that sellers kept lowering their prices. Prices might go down the next day. Buyers and sellers can glance at a chart and get quick visual clues about the direction prices might go.

Stock traders use computers to draw candlestick charts for stocks such as Mattel, Compaq, or Sprint. Unfortunately, computer programs do not generate candlestick charts for collectible CDs. That requires drawing your own candlestick charts.

1. This candle shows what happened to the CD prices during one trading day. Compare the last price of the day to the price at the beginning of the day. If you were selling CDs, would you likely get a better price or a worse price the next trading day? _____

2. This candle shows what happened to the CD prices on another trading day. Imagine that you had sold nearly all of your stash of CDs and wanted to buy more. You intend to resell those for higher prices. On the day after this black candle, would you likely be buying CDs for a cheap price from other sellers or selling your remaining CDs to other buyers? _____

3. This candle and its shadow show what happened to CD prices one trading day. Write a description of what happened to prices during that trading day.

   _____
   _____
   _____

4. This candle and its shadow show what happened to the CD prices one trading day. Write a description of what happened to prices during that trading day.

   _____
   _____
   _____

Song and Culture Go Together

Authors sometimes organize nonfiction by comparing and contrasting. In this article, the author compares a specific style of singing to other styles. As you read the article, notice the comparisons the author makes.

You tune the car radio to your favorite station. Your father backs out of the driveway and then switches the radio back to his oldies station. You groan. You and your dad do not share the same musical culture.

Singing styles vary from one culture to another and from one period in time to another. In societies such as ours, singers tend to prefer wordy solo songs. In more primitive cultures people often prefer to sing together, rather than solo. In one culture—that of the Tuva of Siberia—a single person can sing the part of two people. The throat-singers of Tuva sing a series of flutelike sounds at the same time that they are producing a droning, sustained sound.

Although a few Western singers can produce similar effects, most find the technique impossible. There must be something different about the throats and vocal chords of the Tuva people, some listeners concluded. However, researchers Theodore Levin and Michael Edgerton discovered that the Tuva people produce these simultaneous sounds by using the same techniques other people use to form vowel sounds. The throat-singers are just better at shaping their sounds. They also manipulate the positions of their jaws and lips and have learned to vibrate other structures in their throats.

The Tuva people also live in the perfect place to perfect their technique. Open grasslands allow them to practice making sounds, a self-taught skill. On the open grasslands, the Tuva people hear the buzzing, whistling, twittering sounds of nature. The droning and flutelike tones of the singers mimic these natural sounds.

Herders spend the most time on the open grasslands. This may explain why many throat-singers are herders. Since herders rank low in Tuva society, it becomes apparent why many Tuva people considered throat-singing commonplace and not a worthy art form. Also, few women worked as herders, perhaps accounting for the fact that few throat-singers are women. Song styles reflect the culture of Tuva, just as they do in our own society.

Who is your favorite singing star or group? Write the name of that singer or group in the blank space at the top of the chart below. Then fill out the chart, comparing and contrasting a Tuva singer with your favorite star or group. Think about culture, gender, voice training, singing style, earnings, and other matters related to their singing.

Tuva Throat-singer	_____

Name _____

Tracking Down a Friend

You have just moved. It is your birthday and someone left a gift on your doorstep. There is no card, but your anonymous friend left a clue behind—folded up directions to your house. Here's a map of your new neighborhood with X's at the homes of your three new friends. Follow the printed directions **backwards** to find the identity of the person who left the gift.

Your Friend's Printed Directions:
1. Start out going WEST towards AUTUMN LAUREL TRAIL. Go 50 meters.
2. Turn RIGHT onto AUTUMN LAUREL TRAIL. Go 280 meters.
3. Turn RIGHT onto HIGHLAND FARMS ROAD. Go 400 meters.
4. Turn RIGHT onto ROYAL GARDEN DRIVE. Go 200 meters.
5. Turn LEFT onto SHANGRILA LANE. Go 160 meters to your destination.

Which new friend left the gift? _____

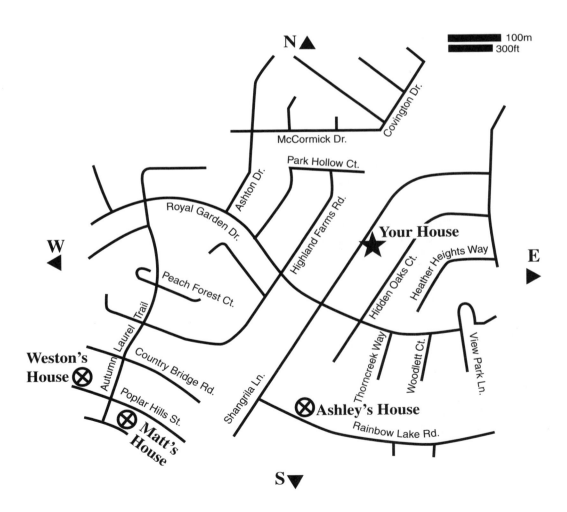

Name _____

Nissen Gets a Job

This reading selection contains words in bold type. These words possess more than one meaning. Two alternate meanings follow each word in bold type. As you read the passage, mentally substitute each alternate word or phrase. Underline the one that best matches the meaning of the word in bold type as it is used in this article.

What **bears** (carries, endures) the name of a trapeze artist but was invented by a gymnast? The trampoline.

Actually, the Eskimos invented the first form of the trampoline. They used a sea lion skin to throw each other into the air. Du Trampolin, a trapeze artist, borrowed their idea, creating a trapeze safety net. However, it was George Nissen, National Tumbling Champion from 1935–1937, who invented the modern form of the trampoline.

Nissen **maintains** (keeps in good order, claims) that his father had asked him to get a real job. Nissen preferred working on his newest project. He had **spotted** (dotted, seen) circus performers using the trampoline to propel themselves into the air, and he decided that gymnasts could do the same. He experimented and produced a working model of the first modern trampoline.

His father still thought he needed a real job, but Nissen had other ideas. He traveled, demonstrating his trampoline to school students and their gym teachers. Soon he began to get orders, but still he wasn't **drawing** (collecting, sketching) a big salary.

Then came World War II. Nissen **imagined** (supposed, fancied) that his small business would **fold** (collapse, crease). The military needed all the available rubber and metal. It was about then that Nissen obtained his first big order—from the military. The Navy **employed** (hired, used) the trampoline to train pilots. The trampoline allowed the pilots to experience weightlessness, if only for a few seconds.

By the time World War II ended, Nissen was ready to start the Nissen Trampoline Company. Nissen's career as an inventor and sports and fitness consultant had just begun. He would eventually **hold** (possess, grasp) more than 30 patents in sports and fitness equipment. Awards would be granted to him and to other athletes in his honor. Nissen finally had a real job, one he had fashioned out of his own enthusiasm and **vision** (sight, imagination).

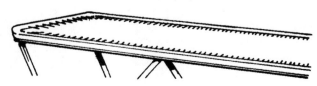

Doctor Anna

As you read the following selection, think about the author's viewpoint toward Doctor Anna. Is that viewpoint supported by details and facts? What assumptions does the author make? Are all the viewpoints the author's, or are some Doctor Anna's?

Anna Pierce Hobbs Bigsby was one determined woman.

In the early nineteenth century, women performed most of the nursing at home, but Bigsby wanted to do more than nurse. She wanted to be a doctor. She soon discovered that few medical schools admitted women. When she finally located a school that would accept her, the school limited the courses she could take. Fortunately, no school could limit her curiosity and determination.

When Doctor Anna returned home to serve her community, milk sickness swept through Southern Illinois. People and animals fell victim. They walked stiffly, trembled, and sometimes died. Doctor Anna's mother and sister-in-law died during the epidemic. So did Abraham Lincoln's mother, who also lived in Southern Illinois.

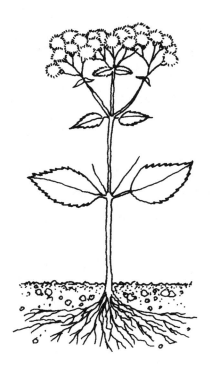

Many blamed witches for the illness, but legend tells that Doctor Anna did not listen to such silly ideas. She began investigating. Milk sickness always hit in summer and stopped after the first frost. Although cattle, horses, goats, sheep, and swine sometimes came down with milk sickness, cattle got it more often. Could milk sickness be caused by something that cattle ate during the summer? Could people contract the illness by drinking tainted milk or eating tainted meat?

Some say that Doctor Anna kept asking that question until someone gave her an answer. A Shawnee woman revealed that the cattle were eating white snakeroot. The Shawnee woman thought that the plant caused the problem. Doctor Anna investigated and found that white snakeroot grew in the areas where milk sickness occurred most often. She convinced the community to get rid of the plants. Many lives were saved.

Most resources do not list Doctor Anna's name, but she probably did not set out to become famous. She was determined to stop people from dying of milk sickness, and that is what she did.

1. How would you describe the author's viewpoint toward Anna Pierce Hobbs Bigsby?

   _____

   _____

2. How does the author support this viewpoint? Name at least two details or supporting statements.

   _____

   _____

3. What unstated beliefs might the author hold about women's difficulties in attending medical school in the early nineteenth century?

   _____

   _____

4. The author writes that Doctor Anna did not listen to such silly ideas. Whose viewpoint was it that it was silly to blame witches for milk sickness?

   _____

Name _____

Young Inventors

If you are learning to play the guitar, you might have reason to thank Nicholas Ravagni. Ravagni owns a patent that helps new guitar players figure out where to place their fingers.

Ravagni collected his patent when he was 11. He got the idea for his invention when he was only six. He designed a self-adhesive and color-coded strip of plastic that fits under a guitar's strings. Ravagni markets the device in music stores and on the Internet.

You can thank other young inventors for some of the products you use every day. If you open your refrigerator, you can probably find leftovers wrapped in aluminum foil. Thank Charles Hall. Hall was a college student in the 1880s when he began experimenting with a process to create a cheap and ready supply of aluminum.

When you tune in to your favorite FM radio station, thank Edwin Armstrong. Just after the turn of the century, Armstrong read a book about inventions. Only 15, he decided that he would become an inventor of radios. He began right away. By the time he was in his early twenties, he had made the first of the discoveries that would lead to his development of the FM radio.

If Hall and Armstrong were still alive, they would probably advise children and teens to have faith in their own abilities. Ravagni would go further. He advises adults to listen to children and teens with good ideas.

Below are some facts and some opinions about the young inventors discussed above. Write F for fact or O for opinion. Remember that a fact can be either true or false but is still a fact even if it can be proved to be false. An opinion can be valid but cannot be proved true or false in the same way a fact can be.

_____ 1. Nicolas Ravagni collected his first patent when he was 11.

_____ 2. Hall experimented with a process to create a cheap and ready supply of aluminum.

_____ 3. Edwin Armstrong's determination to be an inventor led to his success.

_____ 4. If Hall and Armstrong were still alive, they would want children and teens to have faith in their own abilities.

_____ 5. Ravagni advises adults to listen to children and teens.

Name _____

Your Turn to Be an Intern

Imagine that a Web site offers an internship to students your age. Winning one of the internships means that you receive a $5,000 scholarship. Plus you will have the prestige of working for an organization that puts together content about cities and small towns across the United States. As you read the description of the internship, compare and contrast your experiences and abilities with the required experiences and abilities.

As our intern, you will have a unique opportunity to contribute your ideas on teen life in your city. You will help us make the site exciting for teens by suggesting graphics, photography, text, and animation that might appeal to teens. Look over these responsibilities and qualifications and tell us why this job is right for you.

Responsibilities:
Work with both the content and art directors
Develop new sources of content for teens
Choose graphics, photography, text, and animation appropriate for teens
Accurately cover teen-related current events in your city
Juggle several projects at once, meeting multiple deadlines

Qualifications:
Efficient and detail-oriented
Knowledge of your city and teen interests
Strong interest in developing new ideas, while also accepting and fulfilling suggestions from others
Ability to visualize design elements, offering ideas that will appeal to teens and fit into our overall design
Ability to complete work in a timely manner, while balancing several projects

To determine if you have enough qualifications to apply for the internship, fill out the chart. Compare or contrast three responsibilities or qualifications with traits you possess or do not possess.

Responsibilities/ Qualifications	Your Traits

Digging Up the Twenty-First Century

Imagine that you are an archeologist working in the year 3021. You have been digging at the site of an ancient town and you discover a well-preserved structure from the twenty-first century. Inside that structure, you find a windowless room that contains many items. Some appear to be clothing. You also find a rolled-up, glossy, full-colored poster of five young men striding along a beach, each scowling and punching the air with a fisted hand. One drags a stringed instrument behind him. You find three pairs of thick-soled, multi-colored shoes made from some kind of rubbery, elastic material. A blue unstructured object is covered in a shiny material and comes up nearly to your thigh. When you nudge the object with your foot, it appears to be stuffed with small pellets or beads. Those beads shift under your foot, and your foot leaves a dented-in place.

Choose one of those items to study. What can this object tell you about the people living in the twenty-first century? A word or concept map will help you brainstorm. Space for a concept map has been included on the next page. Sketch the item at the top of the page, above the concept map. Put a brief description of the item in the center oval of the concept map. Then jot down ideas about that item as they occur to you, drawing lines to connect ideas that are related to each other. Be inventive. Think about how the item might have been used, why it was constructed as it was, or what it might signify about the society's political or other beliefs. For example, other excavations have turned up hints that many citizens of the twenty-first century suffered hearing losses. Many owned electronic objects that appeared to be worn over the ears, with wires that traveled down to some sort of amplifying device.

Your Sketch

Your Concept Map

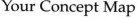

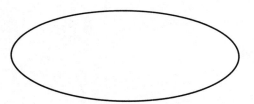

Now that you have finished your word or concept map, write your best conclusion about how the citizens of the twenty-first century might have used the item you studied. Base your conclusion on the most logical ideas drawn from your concept map, which may or may not match the current known use of the item.

_____

_____

_____

Name _____

Mapping Out a Fortune

Authors can use several structures to organize nonfiction. Articles might feature a chronological structure. Events unroll in the order in which they happen. Authors might organize other articles by using cause-and-effect relationships, introducing a problem and solution, or making comparisons between like and unlike things. Even nonfiction articles can use narrative structures, too. They can tell stories about actual events or people.

Sometimes an article might use more than one structure. The opening and closing might present a problem and a solution, for example, while the body of the article employs a narrative structure. Below you will find the first two paragraphs of an article about ancient maps. The opening paragraph uses one structure, while the second uses another. Read each paragraph. Then answer the questions that follow.

Gilbert Bland slipped out of the Peabody Library in Baltimore, unaware that the library's security officers followed him. Bland carried a razor and four 200-year-old maps slashed from rare books. He had already made an estimated half a million dollars by stealing ancient maps, and he intended to sell these maps, too. Bland did not know it yet, but he was about to be caught.

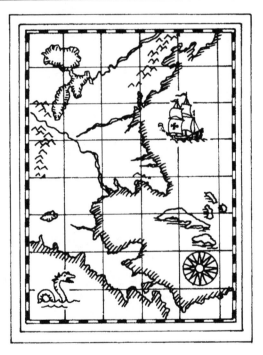

What makes ancient maps so much more valuable than modern maps? Old maps are rare, while modern maps are not. Unlike today, mapmaking took so much effort that mapmakers could produce only a few at a time. Many disappeared during the first few centuries A.D. Their rarity increases their worth because there are not enough maps to satisfy collectors.

1. The opening paragraph uses a
   _____ structure.

2. The second paragraph uses a _____ structure.

3. Since the second paragraph begins the body of the article, the most likely structure for the rest of the body of the article is also a _____ structure.

4. Since the article's opening tells of Gilbert Bland's capture, the author will probably return to the _____ structure for the article's closing, telling of the sentence Bland received or the steps the Peabody Library took to prevent other thefts.

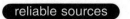

Name _____

E-mail Alert

Internet users across the United States sometimes receive e-mail alerts similar to the one below. These e-mails warn of a possible extra cost or surcharge for e-mail services. As you read the message, notice the source of the information. Is that source reliable or unreliable?

U.S. Representative David McDavid today introduced Bill 409 to the House of Representatives. McDavid reports that Internet e-mail and instant messaging services cost the U.S. Postal Service in lost postage fees. Bill 409 would permit the U.S. Postal Service to charge a five-cent surcharge on each e-mail sent. The U.S. Postal Service would bill the Internet service provider, which would in turn charge the sender of the e-mail. Representative McDavid reports that no final decision has been made on charging for instant messaging services. This surcharge may be added to the bill at a later time. Attorney Ronald Sneed of Omaha, Nebraska, has agreed to fight this bill, filing a class-action suit on behalf of a group of frequent Internet users. Sneed has asked that citizens forward this e-mail to everyone on their mailing list, in order to alert citizens to this new charge.

Write your answers.

1. According to this alert, who is David McDavid? _____

2. According to this alert, who is Ronald Sneed? _____

3. Which statement is true? Put a check by the correct statement.
   _____ The article identifies David McDavid as the source of the information about Bill 409.
   _____ The article identifies Ronald Sneed as the source of the information about Bill 409.
   _____ The article does not identify the source of the information about Bill 409.

4. Name three steps you might take to check out the information in this e-mail.

   _____

   _____

   _____

5. In your opinion, does the proposed surcharge seem logical? Explain your conclusion.

   _____

6. From the information provided here, would you guess that Bill 409 exists or that the e-mail may be promoting a hoax or urban legend?

   _____

Working It Out

Your next-door neighbors own The Plucked Chicken, a local restaurant. They have promised to give you a job as a host after your next birthday. To prepare you for the work, they let you try the job for an evening.

At the restaurant, they hand you a seating chart and a list of suggestions for seating the restaurant's patrons. Familiarize yourself with the seating chart on this page before turning to the seating suggestions on the next page. Tables 111–117 are booths, as are all the tables lining the wall nearest the kitchen. Dotted lines outline the sections for each server. For example, Peter's section includes booths 115, 116, and 117.

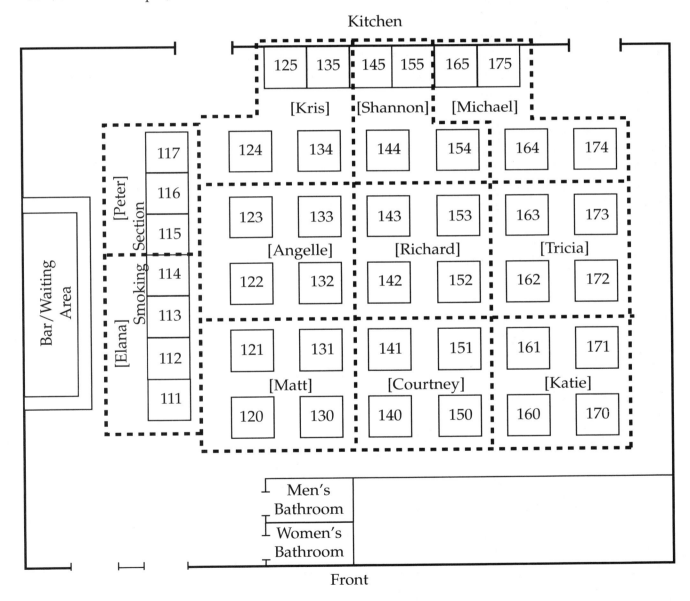

Seating Suggestions for Hosts at The Plucked Chicken

We use a rotation order to make certain that each server gets an equal number of patrons during the evening. Follow the rotation order for seating patrons as closely as possible. When you have to skip one of the servers because of a patron's needs, remember to go back and seat the next patrons in the skipped server's section. The rotation order is as follows:

- Seat patrons using crutches, canes, or walkers near the front of the restaurant.
- Patrons in wheelchairs or families with children who require high chairs should be seated at tables, not booths.
- Families with children between three and ten years old usually prefer booths.
- Groups of men, especially tall men, usually prefer not to sit in booths.
- Couples usually prefer booths.
- Some patrons have a preference for smoking or nonsmoking sections.
- Some patrons ask to be seated in the section of a favorite server, and their wishes take preference to the rotation order.

Now that you have studied the chart and the suggestions, you are ready to begin. Tables 113, 120, 125, and 170 are open. Patrons sit at all other tables.

1. Your first task is to put X's on all occupied tables, so that you will not accidentally try to seat patrons there.

The following patrons arrive, in the order they are listed. Write the table or booth and the server in whose section you seat these patrons. Remember to follow the rotation order when possible. Katie and Peter were the last servers to have patrons seated in their sections.

Nonsmoking Section	Smoking Section
Kris	Elana
Shannon	Peter
Michael	
Angelle	
Richard	
Tricia	
Matt	
Courtney	
Katie	

2. A nonsmoking couple on a first date
   You seat them at _____ in the section
   served by_____.

3. A woman on crutches, accompanied by a man her age, both nonsmokers
   You seat them at _____ in the section
   served by _____.

4. Four businessmen, dressed in suits
   You seat them at _____ in the section
   served by _____.

5. Three women who want to smoke
   You seat them at _____ in the section
   served by _____.

War of the Dictionaries

This article about dictionaries contains some words in bold type. These words use meanings or spellings that once were common but now are unfamiliar. You may be able to figure out the meanings of some words by thinking of a familiar word similar to the word in bold type. Use context and other clues to help you decide on the meanings of these words.

Maybe you consider dictionaries boring. They were not boring in the middle of the nineteenth century, when the war of the dictionaries broke out.

The first **calepin** to include American words and expressions appeared in 1800. Critics immediately attacked it. Many educated people debated the purpose of dictionaries. **Wern** dictionaries supposed to fix language, or should language be fluid and changeable? The new words in the American **tonge** angered those in favor of fixing language.

Noah Webster tried to appeal to both ways of thinking. He introduced *An American Dictionary of the English Language.* In this dictionary, he recognized that the English language was one language across the world. He tried to standardize spellings, but he also introduced American innovations. His ideas did not prove traditional enough for Joseph Emerson Worcester and his followers.

The war of the dictionaries broke out, with Webster's and Worcester's publishers battling each other to sell more copies. Webster and Worcester each wanted his version of the dictionary to be recognized as the most correct version. Each feared that the sales of his version would be **mynished** by the sales of his competitor's version.

In 1860 it looked as if Worcester's version would win. Then in 1864, Webster published a new, more complete dictionary. Somehow, his publisher also convinced a state legislator to state that one of Webster's dictionaries should be placed in every **scoole** in the state.

If you look around your English classroom or school library, you will probably find a Webster's dictionary, complete with **wordes** from American slang. Webster's version won the war of the dictionaries.

Complete the crossword puzzle below by using the currently used word or the current spelling of an old word to fill in the spaces. Use the context clues you discovered to help you decide on the current word.

Across
  2. mynished
  4. tonge
  5. wordes

Down
  1. scoole
  2. calepin
  3. wern

Webster and Worcester argued whether language ought to be fixed and remain the same forever, or whether it ought to be fluid and changeable. Now that you have read this article and completed this crossword puzzle, what is your opinion of the advantages of fixing language versus the advantages of keeping language fluid and changeable? Remember to consider how you would handle newly invented words that describe new developments in technology.

_____

_____

_____

_____

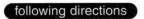

Name _____

Make This

Reading instructions requires careful attention to details. Follow these instructions to make your own origami project.

1. Tear an 8½" x 11" sheet of paper into lengthwise halves. You should have two strips that are each 4¼" x 11" inches. Share one of the strips with a friend.
2. Fold top of strip down 1 inch. Then fold it down another inch.
3. Fold top backwards 1½ inches.
4. Fold bottom up 3¼ inches.
5. Flip folded paper over. You should be looking at the first two folds you made. The folds should make a cuff that turns down.
6. Hold each upper corner of the cuff. Bring those two corners together in the center of the rectangle. The upper edges will now be together in the center of the rectangle. Press the triangular-shaped sides down.
7. Now move your hand out to one outside edge of the rectangle. Fold it in one inch. Do the same on the other edge. The two edges will not meet. You should be able to see the tip of the previous triangular-shaped fold.
8. Start with either of the two folded-in edges. Press your finger on the inside layer of the folded-in edge to hold it in place. Push the other layer back out to its original position. The top of the two layers will begin to fold down. Complete that fold, forming another triangle shape at the top of the opened-out fold. Repeat the process for the other edge.
9. Now grasp the top of the paper, folding it back about 1 inch. Fold the single layer at the back up about 1 inch, so that it now touches the top of the folded papers.

You have completed your project. What is it? Circle the drawing that looks like the origami project you have made.

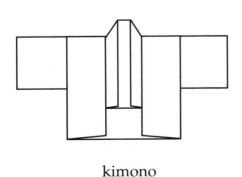

kimono

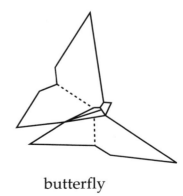

butterfly

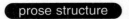

Name _____

Working Canines

Authors sometimes structure articles by introducing a problem and then offering a solution. "Working Canines" uses this structure, although it does not state the problem outright. When you recognize that an article introduces a problem to be solved, you can study the article for details or facts that might lead to a solution. As you read this article, notice the problem and the solution the article offers.

He once was homeless. He was locked up. Now someone trusts him with an important job.

His name is Nicky, and he is a German shepherd. Because of his hyperactivity, his owners turned him over to a pound. Only a day before he was scheduled to die, a German shepherd rescue group found him and sent him to work in the Coast Guard's canine program.

People and dogs have a long history of working together—10,000 to 20,000 years. Dogs work as entertainers. They work in search and rescue and as helping dogs for people with disabilities. They herd and hunt, and they assist police and military units.

Through those long years of working with humans, many dog breeds developed characteristics that helped in their tasks. A retriever's high energy level helps this dog serve people with disabilities or forage through rough country, retrieving game. A border collie's intelligence helps it keep a herd together. The hyperactivity that caused Nicky so much trouble in his first home actually benefits him now in his active work with the Coast Guard. He climbs and scoots through tight spaces on ships.

Nicky almost died because of his behavior problems, but all he really needed was some work to do.

Write your answers.
1. What main problem does the article introduce?

   _____

2. What solution does this article offer?

   _____

3. List two facts or details that support that solution.

   _____

   _____

Name _____

Archeologists Working Here

Archeologists study the remains of other human civilizations. When they discover a bit of pottery or a tool, they often consider what they already know about the civilization that produced the item. They use what they already know as well as what they notice about the object to interpret the new discovery. Sometimes when you read a selection, you might already know something about the topic. Illustrations might help you form ideas about what might be discussed. The title can give you clues. Your prior knowledge of the topic can help you form expectations of what you can learn when reading the selection.

Follow these directions and then write your answers.

1. The reading selection on the next page discusses the working conditions of archeologists. Do not turn the page yet. First, look at the illustration on this page. Think about what you already know about the working conditions of archeologists. Then write a few notes, telling what you already know about this topic along with what you might have learned from looking at the illustration.

   _____

   _____

   _____

   _____

2. What do you expect to learn when reading the selection on the next page? Write two questions that you think might be answered in the reading selection.

   _____

   _____

Not Just Poking Around

The man and woman creep forward. The man toes the leaf mulch covering a pile of rubble, listening for the rustle of snakes. Sweat pools in the creases around his neck. The woman spots something in the rubble. It's a bit of pottery.

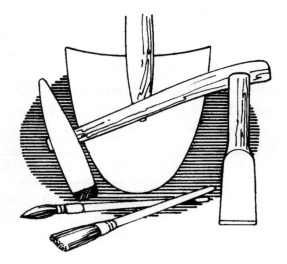

These people work as archeologists. They excavate or dig up the remains of other cultures, and their working conditions can be harsh. Many archeologists teach at universities during the winter. They dig during the summer, so they often dig in fierce heat. Sites may be isolated, without the comforts most of us take for granted. If excavations take place in caves, as did one expedition to the caves of the Chiapas region of Mexico, archeologists must be healthy enough to climb difficult terrain. Animals sometimes threaten archeologists—including human animals. Some digs take place in countries where terrorists kidnap foreigners.

Governments sometimes cooperate with a dig or sometimes ban archeologists from returning to a site. Sponsors sometimes withdraw the funds for a dig. If all that was not enough, fellow archeologists might dismiss an archeologist's findings after all this work.

Still, there must be something about archeology that transcends all these hardships. Archeologist Thomas Lee helped excavate caves hundreds of feet above a river in Chiapas, Mexico, while in his mid-60s. Archeologist Ian Hodder spent six summers in south-central Turkey, working in harsh conditions, and plans to return there every summer for the next two decades. Like other archeologists, these men have faced snakes, heat, and the doubts of other archeologists, and still they are driven to continue their work.

Write your answers.
1. On the previous page, you wrote two questions about this topic. If the article provided answers to those questions, write the answers.

   _____

   _____

2. Write two new things you learned about the working conditions for archeologists after reading this selection.

   _____

   _____

A Scary Business

Recognizing cause-and-effect relationships can help you understand why certain events happened. The cause explains why an event happened. The event is the effect. Words such as *because* or *since* provide clues that one event caused another to occur, but articles do not always include those clue words. When you read the article below, look for clue words, also asking yourself what happened and why it happened. When you finish the article, turn to the next page and answer the questions about cause and effect.

It was nearly two a.m. in Gatesville, Texas, in 1949. Three men stood around a table that held a human skull. Metal instruments and beads of plastic littered the table.

This scene does not portray a police investigation of a strange murder case. It portrays a business being born. Two of the men were brothers and doctors. Because they had not been able to find the human skeletons they needed to teach their students, they had decided to start a company to reproduce human skeletons. The third man was a dentist, Dr. Tom Williams. As a dentist, Dr. Williams had often made molds of his patients' teeth. The brothers thought he would be a valuable addition to their new business.

Dr. Williams told an interviewer in the *Houston Chronicle* that in the beginning he was not certain that the business would work. The United States limited the trade of actual human bones. Where would they get the bones to cast? Still, he was willing to try.

He and the two doctors practiced by casting chicken bones. Just as Dr. Williams thought, the three ran into all kinds of problems. They worked long hours before they perfected the process. They went into debt.

Dr. Williams still had doubts, but he kept going. Gradually the three men began making a profit. They learned how to reproduce organs and other structures, too. By the turn of this century, they produced plastic bodies or limbs that appeared broken, bloodied, or burned. Realistic, plastic internal organs could be removed from skeletons. On some plastic torsos, IVs could be administered and blood could be drawn. Medical and rescue personnel could practice emergency procedures.

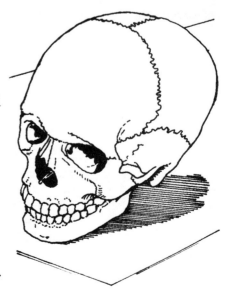

Dr. Williams had not been certain that the new company would work, but by the turn of this century, his company employed 130 people. More importantly, medical students everywhere benefited from his willingness to give the business a try and to keep going, even when he had doubts.

1. What caused the two doctors to begin the business?

   _____

2. What was the effect of producing torsos from which artificial blood could be drawn?

   _____

3. How did the limitation on the trade of human bones impact the two doctors who started the business?

   _____

Below are a series of paired causes and effects. Read each pair of sentences. Then write cause or effect in the space beside each sentence in the pair.

_____ 4. The business eventually employed 130 people.

_____ Dr. Williams kept going, despite his initial doubts about the business.

_____ 5. Dr. Williams had experience making molds of patients' teeth.

_____ The two doctors asked Dr. Williams to join their business.

_____ 6. The United States restricted trade in human bones.

_____ Dr. Williams had doubts about the new business.

_____ 7. Medical and rescue personnel could practice emergency procedures.

_____ The men learned how to reproduce organs and other structures.

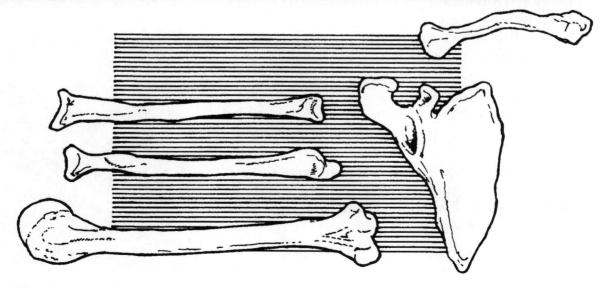

No Apple a Day

The following article discusses astronauts' diets. It includes specialized words in bold type. If any of these words appear unfamiliar, look for clues to their meanings. The text might include a definition or explanation. It might include examples that help you understand the specialized words. It might include a description.

If you are a vegetarian and plan to be an astronaut, you might long for fresh foods during long-term space travel. Those fresh vegetables and fruits might be in short supply.

On long space flights, astronauts must eat all fresh fruits and vegetables within a few days, before they spoil. **Rehydrated, thermostabilized, intermediate-moisture,** and **natural** foods make up the bulk of an astronaut's diet.

You probably eat some **rehydrated** foods at home. You have probably added water to dried soup in a cup and then heated it. **Thermostabilized** foods may appear even more familiar. Astronauts eat canned tuna that tastes like the tuna you have at home, for example. The only difference is that packagers heat their tuna to kill any microorganisms or enzymes that might be present. **Intermediate-moisture** and natural-form foods might also prove familiar. Examples of intermediate-moisture foods include dried fruits and beef. These foods hold only enough moisture to keep them soft. **Natural** foods include nuts, cookies, and granola bars, among other foods. Astronauts also favor tortillas, in addition to the other natural foods. These breads do not produce the crumbs that other breads do. In the past crumbs caused problems for astronauts, fouling their instruments.

If canned and packaged foods make up the bulk of your diet, go ahead and apply for space travel. If you are a fresh-apple-a-day kind of person, maybe another career might be best.

1. Match each specialized word or term with an example of a food that might belong to that category by placing the correct letter in the blank.

_____ Rehydrated foods

_____ Thermostabilized foods

_____ Intermediate-moisture foods

_____ Natural foods

a. canned foods that have been heated to keep them from spoiling

b. partially dried foods to which no water is added before eating

c. foods eaten in their natural form

d. dried foods to which water is added before eating.

How would you classify the following foods? Write R for rehydrated, T for thermostabilized, IM for intermediate-moisture, or N for natural foods.

_____ 2. canned tomatoes and eggplant

_____ 3. candy-coated peanuts

_____ 4. crackers

_____ 5. dried beef

_____ 6. dried rice and chicken soup

7. On a recent nine-day space flight, NASA's menu for one astronaut included fresh carrots. Were those carrots more likely included on the first day's menu or the eighth day's menu? State the reason for your conclusion.

_____

_____

_____

_____

Name _____

Mind Your (Animal) Manners

To fully understand nonfiction, think about the conclusions the author reaches. Are they logical? Read the following article, thinking about the conclusions the author makes. Draw conclusions after thinking about the details or facts in the selection.

Even chimps learn manners. In one group, chimps stamp their feet to get attention. If they join a second group, they might be frowned at for that behavior. In the second group, chimps might knock their knuckles together to get attention.

Most people think of culture as the art, music, or literature of a group of people. Culture includes more. It includes behaviors and ways of life. Those behaviors can differ from society to society. Scientists are discovering that animals have culture, too, and that members of an animal group often teach others their culture. For example, one researcher taught primates to wash food before eating. When the females had babies, they passed this new behavior on to their infants, rearing a new generation of food-washers.

Even in the wild, culture exists. After a fight, female chimps hold grudges, but older males teach younger ones postures and gestures that show that they are ready to make peace. Many of us need to learn those kinds of manners!

Write your answers.

1. Did scientists always know that animals had culture? What conclusion would you draw?_____

   What statement from the reading selection supports your conclusion?

   _____

2. Does the author conclude that animals learn their culture or that animals inherit their culture? _____

3. After reading this selection, draw a conclusion about the purpose of culture in animals._____

   What assumptions did you make in order to draw your conclusion?

   _____

Name _____

Dog Manners

Scientists claim that animals have culture, too. Some might say that animals have manners. Animal manners probably smooth relationships among animals, just as manners smooth our relationships with each other. After you have solved the puzzle on this page, you will read a sentence that describes one of the ways dogs smooth their relationships with each other. Solving the puzzle requires careful attention to directions.

The puzzle spells out a sentence about dog manners. A computer program dropped all the letters you will need below the puzzle. Each letter remains in the same column in which it appears in the puzzle, but the letters have been scrambled within the column itself. To solve the puzzle, think first about the main idea of the puzzle, and scan the letters for words you might expect to find in a puzzle about dogs and their manners. Then you will unscramble the letters in each column, putting them back into the correct position in that column so that the words make sense.

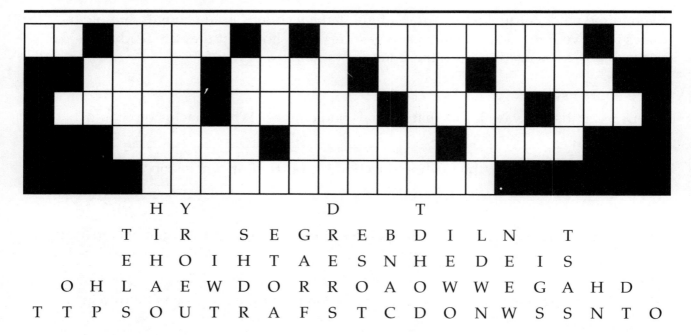

They Can't Help It

Generalizations make statements about a group of people or things. *Most students in the United States attend public schools* is a generalization. Words such as *most, always*, and *never* offer clues to generalizations. Read the following article and look for clue words that indicate that the author might be making generalizations.

The bell rings for the next period. "You forgot to give us homework!" a student in the front row cries.

That's probably a firstborn asking for homework. Researcher Frank J. Sulloway found most firstborns respectful of authority. They can be pretty bossy and authoritarian themselves, but only because they want to keep things going smoothly. They can be reformers, too. They often lead fashionable or socially acceptable reforms. For example, many firstborn baby boomers led movements that cracked down on drugs and cigarette smoking.

Laterborns have to compete for parental attention. That's not bad, Sulloway claims. Laterborns learn tolerance and openness to new ideas. They often begin new movements in science and politics and do not worry whether they are socially acceptable movements. For example, laterborns helped start the French Revolution.

Middleborns play an important role in science and politics, too, according to Sulloway. Most are good at refereeing. They ease cooperation between groups.

In your generation, the average family consists of fewer than two children. When family size decreases, a higher proportion of children are firstborns. Fewer children are middleborns. Family size decreased in the Depression of the 1930s, too, and that generation grew up to defend and accept authority.

Will your generation do the same? Probably, but not necessarily. You probably know firstborns who challenge authority, middleborns who never cooperate, and laterborns who follow rules. Galileo and Einstein, two firstborns, developed bold, creative ideas about science. Exceptions exist, but other studies confirm that birth order influences behavior. So, all you laterborns, please excuse the rule-following, authority-loving firstborns asking for more homework. Ask the middleborns to referee if anyone gets too mad about it.

Write your answers.

1. Are you a firstborn, middleborn, or laterborn? Using the article as a guide, write a generalization about people who share your birth order. How do you differ from that generalization? _____

_____

Examples or facts can help you decide whether a generalization is valid. Sometimes authors make invalid generalizations. For example, if exceptions exist, a statement that something always or never happens is an invalid generalization.

Read the following generalizations about birth order. Based on the information you read in "They Can't Help It," write V for valid or I for invalid.

2. _____ Most firstborns follow rules.

3. _____ Laterborns are always more tolerant than firstborns.

4. _____ Middleborns tend to be more cooperative than firstborns.

5. _____ Firstborns never start new political movements.

6. _____ When family size decreases, the new generation has fewer middleborns.

Read these generalizations. Decide which group of people or events is being described. Then fill in the blank with the correct answer.

7. Most had fewer children than in previous generations. This generalization applies to _____.

8. Many lead political movements to preserve the status quo. This generalization applies to _____.

9. They proposed some of the world's most radical ideas in science or politics. This generalization applies to _____.

10. They often relate well to adults because they tend to respect authority figures. This generalization applies to _____.

Name _____

Cookie Spies

Do you know about Internet cookies? Computer programmers create tools called *cookies*. They track visitors to Internet sites. Cookies report all kinds of information back to companies. You might feel that they violate your privacy.

To find out how companies protect or abuse your privacy, check their privacy statements. The next page includes the privacy statements of two Internet companies. Read those statements before answering the questions on this page. The statements will prove challenging to read, so you will need lots of reading strategies. Think about how each fact relates to cookies and Internet privacy. Break long, difficult sentences into separate ideas. Grasp each idea before attempting to understand the whole sentence. Read slowly and reread passages when necessary. You can do it.

After reading the privacy statements on the next page, answer these questions that compare and contrast the privacy policies of the two companies. To answer, fill in the blank with *Both companies, Neither company, MadeUpCompany 1,* or *MadeUpCompany 2.*

_____ 1. use(s) cookies to track your purchases.

_____ 2. use(s) cookies to remember sign-in or login information.

_____ 3. share(s) information with partners.

_____ 4. control(s) what happens to your information once you click on a banner ad.

Write T for true, F for false, or U for unable to determine from the privacy statement.

_____ 5. MadeUpCompany 1 does not include your name in the information it uses to target ads, promotions, and other marketing messages.

_____ 6. If you make a purchase from MadeUpCompany 1, you may begin getting promotional messages from some of its partners.

_____ 7. Even if you do not make a purchase from MadeUpCompany 2, your information may be shared with its partners.

_____ 8. Both sites supervise the privacy policies of other companies before they allow them to place banner ads.

_____ 9. MadeUpCompany 2 does not share your name with its partners.

MadeUpCompany 1

Cookies

We use cookies to keep track of your shopping cart. We also use cookies to send you information that might interest you and to save your password so that you do not have to reenter it each time you visit our site.

Order Form

When visitors to our site request information, products, or services, we collect contact information, such as e-mail addresses. When products or services are ordered, we also collect financial information, such as account and credit card numbers. We need contact information to get in touch with visitors or to send orders or information. We also provide this contact information to some of our partners, who may send promotional material to our customers. Users can stop these mailings by sending a request via e-mail. We use financial information to bill the user for products and services but do not provide this information to our partners.

Advertisements

This site uses a service to tailor ads, promotions, and other marketing messages to the interests of the site visitors. This service collects data through the use of cookies but does not collect the names of site visitors. Cookies received with banner ads are collected by our advertising company, and we do not have access to this information.

MadeUpCompany 2

To establish your user identification number, you will provide your name, e-mail address, phone number, and address. The process also requests information on your interests. Cookies are then used to track your login information and to allow you to move around the site.

When you use this site to click through to other online retailers, we store referral information so that we may track this with our partners. We share all your provided user identification information with our partners, and by using this service, you consent to the collection and use of your information.

When you click on links or banners that take you to third-party Web sites, you will be subject to the third parties' privacy policies. We cannot be responsible for their actions.

Name _____

Practice, Practice

Details in illustrations and photographs help you draw conclusions about the people, scenes, or events being shown. Those conclusions might influence how you react to those people, scenes, or events. Study the details in the illustration on this page. The questions below ask you to draw conclusions based on the details you see in the illustration. Fill in the blank with the letter representing the best answer.

_____ 1. The people in this illustration are probably . . .
    a. about the same age.
    b. of widely differing ages.

_____ 2. The people shown in this illustration are probably . . .
    a. beginners just learning to play a musical instrument.
    b. members of a marching band.

_____ 3. These people are probably . . .
    a. participating in a marching band competition or performance.
    b. practicing for a marching band competition or performance.

_____ 4. This event probably is happening . . .
    a. on a warm day.
    b. on a crisp fall day.

_____ 5. These people probably . . .
    a. make up the entire band to which they belong.
    b. are just one section of a larger marching band.

_____ 6. These people probably took their places . . .
    a. according to a plan or design they are learning to follow.
    b. according to height.

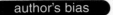

Name _____

Pig Transplants

In this article, the author asks you to play the part of a doctor making a medical decision. To make that decision, you would weigh the risks against the benefits. Before making judgments based on the material you read, it is important to notice whether the author's presentation of the material is a balanced one. Balanced writing includes all the sides of an argument. Do you have all the information you need to make a judgment? Think about these issues as you read the article.

You're a doctor. Your patient has been involved in a terrible automobile accident. He has lost so much skin on his leg that you fear that the leg will have to be amputated. You have heard about a new material called SIS. When doctors place SIS over a wound, the patient's own skin grows back. The SIS disappears within two or three months, and no infection or rejection occurs.

What's the catch? Scientists harvest SIS from the small intestines of pigs.

Pigs' intestinal walls contain several layers. SIS makes up the submucosa, a layer sandwiched between the inner layer and the muscular outer layer. Using a pig's intestinal wall sounds gross, but grossness is not the problem. Some medical ethicists worry that the pigs' tissue might transfer disease to humans, spreading an epidemic. That is probably not a problem with SIS, since scientists treat it with acid and then sterilize it, but it may be a problem with other tissues harvested from pigs. New research shows that doctors soon could transplant pig hearts or kidneys into humans who might die without the new organs. These organs cannot be treated in the same way SIS can. The spread of diseases may be more of a problem with organ transplantation.

Most researchers say that the risks remain small. Some medical ethicists claim that the benefits outweigh the risks: a life or a limb saved versus a small hypothetical risk of disease. If the decision were yours, what would you do?

Write your answers.
1. The author omits any discussion of the ethics of killing animals to benefit humans. Why do you think the author omitted that discussion? _____

   _____

2. In your opinion, does the author present balanced or unbalanced writing? Support your opinion, based on what you notice about the article. _____

   _____

Name _____

They Already Know Your Name

Summarizing a reading selection helps you understand the selection. A summary condenses the selection to its most important points. It avoids retelling or paraphrasing the selection. Read the following selection, thinking about the main idea and the important supporting points.

You have just arrived home from school when the telephone rings. A woman greets you by name. "How's eighth grade going?" she asks.

"Okay," you answer. You do not recognize the woman's voice, but you would not want to be rude to one of your mom's friends. The woman asks whether you are going to homecoming. She offers to order a homecoming mum for you. All she needs is your mom's credit card number.

You are wise enough to realize that you should not give out the credit card number, and the call ends. The woman was not your mom's friend. She was a telephone solicitor. You and your mom wonder how the woman knew your name, school, and grade.

Most likely, the school sold your information to a telemarketing company. Your name, grade, date of birth, address, photographs from the yearbook, and even awards are public record. Federal law requires schools to give that information to anyone requesting it. Even a noncustodial parent can request the information.

Other establishments give out information, too. Your parents' insurance company shares information with other insurance companies. If you took medication for epilepsy when you were five, that information might be available to your mother's insurance company at her new job. Stores and pharmacies track purchases and sell that information to other retailers.

What can you do? You can mark "no" in the records release form your school sends out at the first of each year. Your personal information will not be given out, but you also will not receive some of the same mailings your classmates do. When you are in high school, for example, you might not get college scholarship information. You can also avoid filling out Internet surveys or contest forms. You know not to give out your address, for example, but also avoid telling your favorite movies, your pets' names, and other personal information. Ask your movie rental store about its privacy policy. Do not participate in a telephone survey. Keep a list of any Internet or phone contacts so you can report abuses. Consider not using a grocery store card when you slip in to make a few purchases for your parents. Take steps to protect your privacy.

Write a summary of two to three sentences. _____

_____

_____

Imagine that a telephone solicitor tricks you into believing that she is a friend of your parents. She offers to order a homecoming mum for you. She has not told you her name, but she knows your name, so you think everything is okay. Your mom must have asked her to call. Confused, you mistakenly give her your mother's credit card number. The homecoming flowers never arrive and you forget about your mistake—until your mother's next credit card bill arrives. The bill includes a charge for $59.93 from Anazm Marketing. As punishment, your mother makes you fill out the Federal Trade Commission's Complaint Form. Complete as much of the form as you can, writing *not available* in spaces where you do not know the requested information.

Subject of Your Complaint: _____

Name of Company You Are Complaining About: _____

Address of Company: _____

Company Web Site: _____

Company E-Mail Address: _____

Company Phone Number: _____

How Did the Company Initially Contact You? _____

How Much Did the Company Ask You to Pay? _____

How Did You Pay the Company? _____

How Much Did You Actually Pay the Company? _____

Name of Company Representative or Salesperson

Who Contacted You: _____

Date Company Contacted You: _____

Explain Your Problem: _____

_____

_____

You do not have enough information to help the Federal Trade Commission contact Anazm Marketing. Name two ways you might try to find at least some of the missing information.

_____

_____

Name _____

Genetic Basis of Behavior

You have almost finished your homework. Your last assignment is to write a brief paragraph on any aspect of genetics. You have found an article on the Internet, but it is two pages long, and you are too sleepy to read it.

Do not worry. Skimming the title and headings gives you basic information about the subject you have chosen. That is all you need for the short paragraph.

Read the title and headings of "Genetic Basis of Behavior," an article found on the following page. Then, without going back to read the entire article, write a brief paragraph relating to the material.

_____

_____

_____

_____

_____

Now imagine that your teacher assigns a more detailed essay, using the same resource material. Go back and read the entire article. Did you grasp the main idea from the title and headings alone? Jot down two or three details from the body of the article that you could add to develop that main idea.

_____

_____

_____

GENETIC BASIS OF BEHAVIOR

Maybe it's not your fault that you didn't clean your room a couple of weeks ago. Maybe your genes made you forget.

Genes May Control Behavior as Well as Physical Traits

Genes control the physical traits you inherit from your parents. Genes control your hair color, eye color, and blood type. Some scientists believe that behavior can be inherited, too. You might possess a combination of genes that makes you shy or outgoing. You might be able to concentrate for longer periods than your classmates because of your genetic makeup.

Some Researchers Applaud the Idea of a Genetic Basis to Behavior

Some researchers welcome these new theories. If an inability to concentrate might have a genetic cause, they reason that new teaching methods might help. If you are too shy to read in front of the class, and classmates understand that this trait has a genetic basis, they might be more understanding.

Other Researchers Worry

Other scientists see problems ahead. What about forgetting to clean your room last week? Did you really forget or were you just feeling too lazy? Perhaps laziness will prove to be an inherited trait, too. If science can identify the genes that cause undesirable behaviors such as laziness, the next step might be manipulating genes to prevent those behaviors. These researchers fear a generation of children programmed to have certain traits. Can you imagine a classroom full of smiling, cooperative, focused students sitting with their hands folded on their desks? That would be boring, certainly, but some also find the idea scary.

The Worries May Be Exaggerated

We humans have always worried about the effects of new scientific developments. For example, the novel *Frankenstein* explored the unexpected consequences of a scientific experiment. That novel was published in 1818, so we have had these worries through several generations. Maybe all that worry has a genetic basis, too!

Name _____

Healing Hearts

Nonfiction sometimes includes debatable statements. You might agree or disagree with these statements. That is what makes them debatable! The author might present facts to support debatable statements, but debatable statements themselves are not facts. As you read this article about open-heart surgery, notice which statements might be debatable.

When David and Blanche Peel married in 1918, tragedy awaited them. Two of their babies would be "blue" babies, babies born with damaged hearts. Their skin appeared bluish because their hearts could not supply enough oxygen to their blood. They soon died.

If David and Blanche had married a few decades later, those babies might have survived. People do not often think of war as being beneficial, but World War II brought about many advances in medicine. Doctors operating on wounded soldiers faced injuries they had never seen. Dr. Dwight Harken was one of those doctors. When soldiers came into his hospital with shrapnel in their hearts, he did not know how to operate on a beating heart. The soldiers would die without the surgery, but surgery would kill them, too. Dr. Harken experimented, eventually discovering a successful technique. That technique proved helpful to patients with one kind of heart valve problem, too.

Harken's technique did not allow more complicated surgeries, such as repairing the hearts of babies, but it taught doctors that heart surgery could be survived. It was a beginning, and from that beginning came new techniques. By the 1950s, when Blanche and David's granddaughter developed a condition that could have required open-heart surgery, doctors were ready.

Review the following statements from the article and write D for Debatable or N for Nondebatable.

_____ 1. The skin of "blue" babies appears bluish because their hearts cannot supply enough oxygen.

_____ 2. If David and Blanche had married a few decades later, their two "blue" babies would have survived.

_____ 3. Doctors operating on wounded soldiers in World War II faced injuries they had never seen.

_____ 4. Harken's technique taught doctors that heart surgery could be survived.

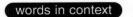

Name _____

Diligent Hero

This article contains words in bold type. Cross out those words and replace them with words or phrases from the list that follows the article. Write the new word or phrase in the spaces provided. To decide on appropriate substitutions, think about the main idea of the selection and of the paragraphs that contain the word. Look at words that come before and after the words in bold type to decide which word would fit into the context.

Sam Boyden probably never expected to **testify** _____ before Congress. Most likely, he never expected to appear on national television, either. Perhaps he never thought he would be called a hero. All those things **transpired** _____ because of his **diligence** _____ in following an insurance case.

Boyden **toiled** _____ in the research unit of an insurance company. One day in July 1998, he got a call about a case. The tread had separated from a tire, causing an accident. Had similar accidents occurred? he was asked. Boyden's **sleuthing** _____ turned up 20 other cases.

Boyden had fulfilled his obligations, but he **persevered** _____. He researched the cases. He found that the same manufacturer had made all the tires involved in the accidents. Two thirds of the accidents involved the same kind of vehicle. Boyden contacted the National Highway Traffic Safety Administration. He persisted in researching similar accidents. When the NHTSA called him back, he was **armed** _____ with information that **documented** _____ _____ the problem.

Boyden did not dive into freezing water to pull out a drowning man. He did not brave a roaring fire. Still, he and the others who identified the problem **achieved** _____ heroic status. Drivers and passengers had already lost their lives in the accidents that occurred when the tire treads separated. Through attention to detail and persistence, Boyden may have helped save many other lives.

Word List

detective work	worked
reached	give evidence
equipped	earnestness
continued	occurred
provided a written account of	

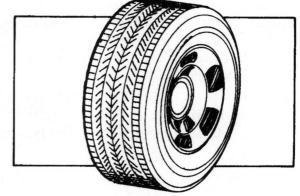

No Regrets for Esther Kim

As you read the following nonfiction selection, think about the author's purpose in writing the selection. Is this selection meant to inform, persuade, or encourage you to experience what Esther Kim experienced? After you read the selection, turn to the next page to answer questions about the author's purpose.

Esther Kim became an Olympic heroine. She did it without competing in the Olympics.

Kim and her best friend, Kay Poe, found themselves in a terrible spot during the Olympic team trials. The 2000 Olympics would be the first Olympics to include tae kwon do as an official sport. Both Kim and Poe were flyweights in tae kwon do. Both won their semifinal matches. They would fight each other for the right to go to Sydney and represent the United States.

Poe had been injured during her semi-final match. A blow to her knee had left the knee so swollen that many doubted that she could compete. Ranked first in the world in her weight class, she probably would lose to Kim.

Kim had different ideas. Tae kwon do athletes learn about courtesy, integrity, perseverance, and self-control. Kim believed that her best friend deserved to compete in the Olympics. When it was time to walk into the ring, she forfeited the fight, giving up her own chance to go to the Olympics.

Although Kim wished that both she and Poe could have competed in the Olympics, she did not regret her choice. She learned that she could do something more difficult than she had ever imagined herself doing. She learned that she was a champion.

1. The author organized this selection around a narrative—the story of the events that led to Kim's forfeiture of the fight. Why do you think the author might use a narrative?

_____

_____

2. What reaction do you think the author was trying to create by involving readers in these events?

_____

_____

3. What unstated belief might underlie the author's view that Esther Kim's actions were heroic?

_____

_____

4. Some people might disagree with the author's unstated belief. Write a statement that would be the opposite of the author's unstated belief.

_____

5. Informative nonfiction informs. It presents facts that might be useful to you in research or in making decisions. Persuasive nonfiction tries to convince readers to accept certain beliefs or act in a certain manner. Entertaining nonfiction sometimes encourages readers to share or participate in someone's experiences. Which of these purposes do you believe prompted this author to write this selection? Support your belief with examples from the article.

_____

_____

_____

_____

Life on Mars

Don't believe everything you read, an ancient proverb advises. That is still good advice. Always check to make certain that an author uses reliable sources. Ask yourself if the information makes sense. Do you need more information to make an informed decision? Read this article about supporting life on Mars, noticing the source of the information. Think about what you already know about the subject. Also draw conclusions about whether the theories discussed in this article seem workable.

Six hundred years from now, an astronaut steps out of her spacecraft onto Martian soil. Her bulky space suit and helmet limit her range of movements, but in Mars' reduced gravity, she bounces toward a garden growing several meters away.

What's wrong with this picture? According to Christopher P. McKay, it's the space suit, not the garden. He envisions a time when scientists can thicken Mars' atmosphere enough to warm the planet and support the growth of plants. In that thickened atmosphere, human colonists would need breathable oxygen, but would not require space suits.

Plants need nitrogen and carbon dioxide. They need water. Many scientists believe that liquid water once ran on Mars. In an article for *Scientific American*, McKay theorizes that water could still be present, frozen as ground ice. The soil could also contain both nitrogen and frozen carbon dioxide. More carbon dioxide could be frozen in Mars' polar caps. Releasing these substances requires warming Mars.

That is why that scene will take place in 600 years. According to McKay, scientists have proposed interesting ideas for warming the planet, but they all require lots of time. Some suggest spreading dark soot on the polar caps, since soot would absorb more of the sun's heat. Some suggest using giant mirrors the size of Texas to focus the sun's heat. McKay does not like those ideas. He suggests an idea that he considers more workable. He proposes transporting little chemical factories to Mars. Chemical reactions would produce greenhouse gases from substances found in Mars' soil. Over a period of 600 years or so, those greenhouse gases would gradually warm Mars' surface, just as they are warming Earth's. Then that astronaut could begin tending to her garden.

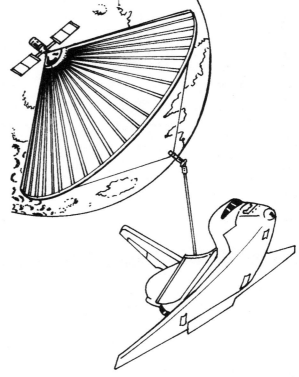

Write your answers.

1. Who is the source of the information that people might not need space suits when visiting Mars in 600 years?

   _____

   What further information would you need about this person to decide whether his theories deserve attention?

   _____

2. What publication included a discussion of Christopher P. McKay's theories?

   _____

   What further information would you need to decide whether this publication's articles are reliable sources of scientific information?

   _____

3. Was it McKay's belief or someone else's that a giant mirror could be used to warm Mars' atmosphere? _____

   What is your opinion of this theory? _____

   _____

4. Which idea does McKay consider the most workable method of warming Mars?_____

   What further information would you need in order to draw an informed conclusion about the practicality of this method?

   _____

5. The author of "Life on Mars" does not provide enough information for you to make informed decisions about all the theories discussed in the article. Still, you can draw some initial conclusions. What can you conclude about the information provided in McKay's article in *Scientific American*?

   _____

   _____

Name _____

The Many Lives of Grace Halsell

Articles sometimes describe a sequence of events, but authors do not always make it easy to sort out the sequence. The author might mention an event but then backtrack to provide the history behind the event. To understand what happened, you must put the events into the correct sequence. Sometimes specific dates or words such as *then* and *next* provide clues. Sometimes readers must make logical decisions about the sequence of events. As you read the following article, pay attention to the sequence of events.

Grace Halsell lived more than one kind of life. She hunted lions. She crossed the Amazon by tugboat. She was the first woman to cover the police beat on the *Fort Worth Star-Telegram.* In the 1960s, she served as the highest-ranking woman on President Johnson's White House staff.

Halsell dared to do more. In 1968 she took pills to darken her skin color. After tanning, she worked as an African American cleaning woman. In the early 1970s, she disguised herself as a Native American and worked as a nanny. In the late 1970s, she crossed the border into the United States, disguising herself as a Mexican migrant worker.

Two events inspired Halsell's efforts to live as minority women did: the 1968 assassination of Dr. Martin Luther King, Jr., and a 1961 book by John Howard Griffin. Griffin had also taken pills to darken his skin. Then he wrote about his experiences. Like Griffin, Halsell wrote about her experiences. She wanted to reveal the prejudice she endured while living as minority women. Her books were translated into six languages and one sold more than one million copies. They created controversy but also helped other people to live more than one life.

Five illustrations follow showing scenes from Grace Halsell's life. Number them from 1–5, with 1 being the earliest and 5 being the last of the sequence.

What would have changed if the events in Grace Halsell's life had occurred out of sequence? For example, if Halsell had not already worked for years as a journalist, she might not have considered it possible to write and sell a book about her experiences. Below you will find questions about the possible consequences if the events in Grace Halsell's life had occurred in a different order. Write your answers.

1. What might have changed if Halsell had not held an important position on President Johnson's White House staff before she approached publishers with her book ideas?

   _____

2. What might have changed if Halsell had worked first as a Native American nanny, rather than first as an African-American cleaning woman? Would this result have impacted her efforts to expose the lives of minority women?

   _____

3. What might have changed in Halsell's life if Griffin had not written his book until 1979?

   _____

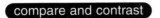
Name _____

A Hard Price

Authors sometimes compare or contrast something new or unfamiliar to something already known. Sometimes clue words such as *like* or *however* signal a comparison or a contrast. Read the following selection, underlining any clue words that signal a comparison or contrast.

You have just finished a solo in your first band concert. Your parents stand and clap. You are embarrassed that they have made such a big deal out of your solo.

Some Ethiopian azmari musicians might envy you. Despite the long tradition behind azmari music, many Ethiopians once despised the azmari musicians. Some of these musicians still must run away from home to play azmari music.

Centuries ago, the azmari performed music to accompany religious ceremonies. Like the minstrels of Medieval Europe, they worked in the courts of the nobles of their society. Also like the European minstrels, they often could not read music. They memorized the music and sometimes improvised, building upon the traditional rules of their music. However, the azmari played instruments unknown in Europe at the time. One was the masenqo, a type of fiddle still played by modern azmari.

The azmari eventually played at other types of occasions. They gradually began singing and playing love poetry and humorous verses. Like European minstrels, they used puns, satire, and humor to mock others, but few minded the mockery.

Now some azmari musicians use new technology to record and market their songs. Reporters and DJs sometimes interview them. They sell CDs. Some achieve success, but some still sacrifice their relationships with their families. These shunned musicians would probably tell you to smile when your adoring but embarrassing parents cheer at the end of the school concert.

Write your answers.
1. The third and fourth paragraphs of this selection make several comparisons between azmari musicians and European minstrels. Name two ways azmari musicians and European minstrels are alike.

   _____

   _____

2. Fill in the blank. The middle of this selection compares and contrasts azmari musicians with European minstrels. The article's opening and conclusion compare and contrast the experiences of azmari musicians with _____

   _____

Name _____

Some Things Never Change

Authors vary their writing styles or voices to achieve different purposes. Read the following selection. Think about the author's purpose and the writing voice the author uses to achieve that purpose.

Your math teacher assigned 45 problems, but before you start on homework, you snack on a wedge of cheese. Then you find a note from your mother. She reminds you that you forgot your volleyball uniform at your friend's house after the last game. You will need it tonight. Your mother also asks you to grate the cheese she left in the fridge for tonight's casserole. Aaagh!

Don't worry. This is the twenty-first century and you live in a big city. Sign onto the Internet and call up one of the new lackey or delivery services.

You arrange to have the uniform picked up and delivered home. While you are online, you notice that the pages load too slowly. Ask the service to send someone to defrag the hard drive and check for viruses. You still need to replace the cheese you ate. You sign onto a home grocery-delivery service, but no delivery times are available until the next day. That is no problem. You sign back onto the lackey service and ask that someone pick up some cheese, too. While you are waiting for the deliveries, you sign onto a homework help site and ask just what on earth a logarithm is, anyway.

Wait. You have forgotten something. The site for homework help does not charge, but someone has to pay for all those other services. It may be the twenty-first century, but some things never change.

Write your answers.

1. The author uses the second person "you" and present-tense verbs in this article. How does this relate to the kind of voice the author was trying to achieve?

   _____

2. This article describes Internet services. Decide whether the author intended to inform you about specific services or to create a feeling that the Internet can be a fun part of modern life. Support your decision.

   _____

   _____

   _____

Virtual Schools

The reading selection below contains words in bold type. These words may be unfamiliar or they may be used in unfamiliar ways. To help you decide what each word means, look for a word you know inside each new word. Also look at context clues.

A 15-year-old gymnast training for the next Olympics. A high-school **freshman** attending a school that does not offer college-preparatory classes. A 12-year-old, full-time actor. What do these people have in common? They attend virtual schools. They read, complete, and **proffer** assignments on the computer.

Scholarship at a distance is not new. Australian children living in the outback often could not attend school. Students and teachers mailed lessons back and forth.

Now computers make it easy for students to learn at a distance, in Australia and elsewhere. **Disabled** or injured students can keep up with their classmates. Students who move through lessons more quickly than their classmates can proceed at their own pace. Students who attend poor or rural schools without higher-level classes can advance. Students with careers in acting or sports can benefit, too. That 15-year-old gymnast can fit schoolwork around workouts.

What **drawbacks** exist? The cost, for one. While U.S. school systems offer free public education, parents often must pay for the online courses, even when local school systems sponsor them. Also, it is up to the student to complete the work on time. Anyone can set up a site, so a school's credentials should be examined closely. Some educators and parents also worry that online students may not **interface** enough with other people their ages.

For many students, the advantages **surpass** the disadvantages. The gymnast, the actor, the disabled student, and the student who needs advanced placement classes might all agree.

Fill in the correct answer, using one of the meanings provided. Use context clues as well as root words to make your decision.

1. As used in this selection, the word *freshman* means _____.
   a. the produce clerk at a grocery store
   b. first-year high school student
   c. a man who tells a lot of rude jokes

2. As used in this selection, the word *proffer* means _____.
   a. grade
   b. submit
   c. teach

3. As used in this selection, the word *scholarship* means _____.
   a. learning
   b. grant money
   c. knowledge

4. As used in this selection, the word *disabled* means _____.
   a. immobilized
   b. halted
   c. physically challenged

5. As used in this selection, the word *drawbacks* means _____.
   a. retreats
   b. sketches
   c. disadvantages

6. As used in this selection, the word *interface* means _____.
   a. interact
   b. argue
   c. boundary

7. As used in this selection, the word *surpass* means _____.
   a. honor
   b. go beyond
   c. stay behind

Sky-High Dreams

Authors often organize articles around a three-part structure: an introduction, a middle, and an ending. The opening hooks readers and reveals the topic of the article. The middle adds details and develops the main idea. The ending reaches a conclusion or sums up the material in the article. After reading the article below, put brackets around each of the three sections of the article. Then answer the questions on the next page.

Young Fred Parks straightened his shoulders and knocked on yet another door. He did not have any money or food, but he did have a vision that he could accomplish something with his life. His first vision was to attend law school. He had taken a job selling advertising to finance that dream.

Selling advertising was not Parks' first job as a salesperson, and it would not be his last. As a child, he had delivered papers and sold produce door-to-door. As an adult, he would work as a lawyer and a real-estate developer, selling office space to businesses.

When in his mid-90s, Parks tackled his biggest selling job. He tried to convince reluctant city governments to adopt his vision of the ideal mass-transit system. In his vision, electric cars, Aerobuses, would run along tracks suspended from 300-foot pylons.

Gerhard Mueller developed the Aerobus system. Parks had first seen it in operation in the 1970s, in a temporary installment. Immediately, Parks envisioned electric cars zipping high above congested city streets, transporting people without producing smog or other pollutants.

Few city governments shared Parks' vision. Finally, he found a city that would consider the Aerobus system. The Chinese metropolis of Chongqing would be the first to adopt the system. Parks might have been in his mid-90s when the construction began, but he still possessed the vision that had driven a young, hungry boy to dream of attending law school.

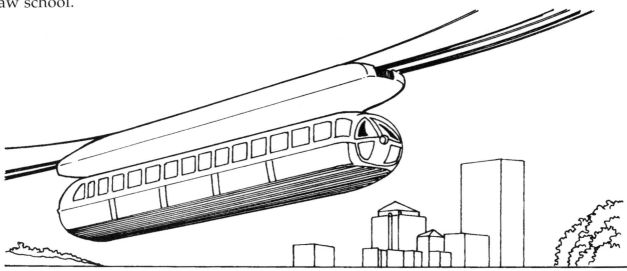

1. This article targets seventh- and eighth-grade readers. The author starts the article with a scene that shows a young Fred Parks. Why would the author begin with a scene that shows a young Fred Parks rather than with a scene that shows the elderly Fred Parks? Write your answer.

   _____

   _____

2. The opening of this article hinted at the article's theme. Circle the theme that the article's opening introduced.

   The Aerobus does not produce much smog or other pollutants.

   Dreams can stir people to overcome obstacles and achieve much.

   Selling advertising is a good way to earn money for school.

   School is necessary if one wants to achieve one's dreams.

3. The third paragraph of this article deals with Parks' attempts to sell the Aerobus system to cities. How does this paragraph relate to the theme of the entire article? Write your answer.

   _____

   _____

4. What conclusion does the author reach in the article's last paragraph? How does that relate to the theme of the article? Write your answer.

   _____

   _____

Name _____

Gesture That Again?

The article below explains why gestures can be confusing from one culture to the next. The article itself proves confusing, because it is scrambled. Read the opening paragraph and predict what comes next. Then test your prediction by finding the next paragraph in the article. Do this for each paragraph until you have put all the paragraphs in the correct order. Number each paragraph after the opening one in the order in which they should appear.

You are on vacation. You have traveled to so many countries that you have lost track of your location. You look at the other diners in the restaurant, but their clothes do not give you any clues. Then your mother leans forward and whispers, "Keep your hands on the table!"

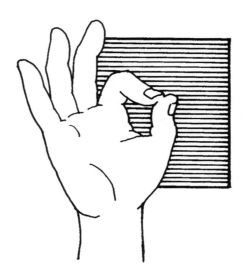

___ Even with Axtel's book in hand, traveling might be confusing. Business travelers sometimes take courses in body etiquette to avoid offending people in the countries they visit. A business traveler to Spain who makes an OK gesture with a circled forefinger and thumb has just offended his hosts!

___ While gestures may differ from country to country, all cultures possess a vocabulary of gestures. Some scientists believe that language developed from the same part of our brains that controls body movements or motor activity. Waving a hand or nodding a head requires movement or motor activity. Speech can be considered a kind of motor activity, too. Just as all humans make similar sounds, we make similar gestures. Different cultures just assign different meanings to those gestures.

___ Aha! Perhaps you have arrived in Bulgaria or Austria. Diners in the United States might be expected to keep their left hands in the laps, but that is just rude in Bulgaria or Austria. Hands stay in sight, on the table.

___ In *Gestures: Do's and Taboos of Body Language Around the World*, Roger Axtel explains that gestures have different meanings in different countries. For example, while you and your friends might nod your heads up and down when you mean "yes," students in Austria signal "yes" by shaking the head from side to side. In Greece, students might tilt their heads to either side to signal "yes," while they might lift their heads slightly to signal "no."

Name _____

An American Icon

As you read this article about the Flatiron Building, use the specific details you encounter to help you visualize the building.

It's old. It's triangular. It's a building that has probably been pictured in more movies that take place in New York than any other building. What is it? It is the Flatiron Building, and it is part of our culture.

Once the tallest building in the United States, the Flatiron Building's 22 floors rise 285 feet. Completed in 1902, experts consider it the oldest remaining skyscraper in New York. After its construction, people across the world admired the Flatiron Building because of its efficient use of a triangular lot, its height, and its beauty. Architect Daniel Burnham and his partner, John Wellborn Root, devised a steel frame structure that allowed buildings to be constructed to greater heights than had previously been possible. Burnham designed the Flatiron Building using their innovations, wrapping it in a rusticated limestone. The narrow end of the building seems to form a classical column. Like a classical column, the building is divided into a beginning, middle, and end. Rows of limestone mark each division. Flowers and Grecian faces decorate the building.

Burnham had a grand vision for architecture. He wanted magic when he designed a building, and he created magic with this one. New York's cityscape would not be the same without this important American icon.

The illustrations to the right feature two buildings designed by Burnham's architecture firm: the Reliance Building and the Flatiron Building. Using details you visualized while reading the article, identify the Flatiron Building. Label each building with the correct name.

_____   _____

The Tale of an Ancient Sailor

Sometimes informational articles contain opinions as well as facts. A statement of fact can be proved true or false. Opinions tell what someone believes to be true. An opinion might be supported by facts, but it cannot be checked and proved true or false in the way a fact can be. Read the following article, thinking about what might be factual and what might be an opinion.

Professor Francesco Mallegni often thinks about the sailor who died clutching his dog. The sailor had raised his right arm. Perhaps he tried to shield himself and his dog from the shifting cargo. Rope had snarled his foot, probably when he returned to the hold to rescue his dog.

The soldier died more than 2000 years ago near the harbor of Pisa, Italy. Thanks to Mallegni and his Italian research team, visitors to a traveling exhibit can look this ancient sailor in the eye. Mallegni and his team developed a computer program that scanned the sailor's skull. His team's computer program accounted for cultural and historical differences in the thicknesses of muscles and skin. Then the program reconstructed the sailor's face.

Already, Mallegni's team has reconstructed the faces of the ancient Roman sailor, a young Egyptian soldier, and an Egyptian prince. Recently, the team reconstructed the face of an ancient Roman man who Mallegni believes to be the famous Italian painter Giotto. The reconstructed face looks like a painting that some think might be Giotto's self-portrait.

These ancient people fascinate Mallegni. The pattern of wear on the teeth of the artist's skull revealed that he had probably held his paintbrush between his teeth. The sailor's skull showed that he was about 40 when he died. The Egyptian soldier's skull revealed that he had probably died of a battle wound. Mallegni thinks that the sailor looks as if he could live in the house next door. Through Mallegni's fascination and attention to detail, these ancient people come alive for today's museum visitors, too.

Name _____

Write F for fact or O for opinion.

_____ 1. Mallegni and his Italian team developed a computer program that helps archeologists reconstruct the faces of ancient people.

_____ 2. The computer program attempts to account for cultural and historical differences in the thicknesses of muscles and skin.

_____ 3. Since the computer program accounts for cultural and historical differences in the thicknesses of muscles and skin, Mallegni's team accurately rebuilds features such as lips and ears.

_____ 4. Visitors to a traveling exhibit can look at Mallegni's reconstruction of the sailor's features.

_____ 5. The ancient sailor was discovered near Pisa, Italy.

_____ 6. The ancient sailor raised his arm to protect himself and his dog from the shifting cargo.

_____ 7. The ancient sailor died clutching a dog.

_____ 8. The ancient sailor's foot was tangled in rope.

_____ 9. The ancient sailor looks as if he could live next door.

_____ 10. The ancient sailor was about 40 when he died.

_____ 11. The Egyptian soldier's skull showed a wound of the kind that might be received in a battle.

_____ 12. The Egyptian soldier died of a wound received in battle.

_____ 13. Mallegni believes that the ancient Roman whose face he reconstructed is the painter Giotto.

_____ 14. Mallegni compared the Roman face he reconstructed to a self-portrait of the painter Giotto.

_____ 15. The pattern of wear on the artist's teeth revealed that he often held his paintbrush between his teeth.

Answer Key

Plan It   **page 5**

Retaining Wall

Truck Loading Ramp

Night Receiving ②

Bakery Storage ⑤ | Freezer Box ③ | Meat Cutting ④ | Meat Storage Box

Rest Room
Rest Room

Bakery Box | Dairy Box | Produce Box ⑥ | Meat Box

Stock Room

Checkout Area

Store Area

① Bottle Storage

⑦ Employee Lounge

Cheap Thrills   **page 6**
1. Students might mention any three of the following comparisons, plus logical comparisons drawn from their own experiences: cheap price, include violence, quickly written, disliked or criticized by many, and sometimes feature inferior writing.
2. Students might make the following two comparisons, plus logical comparisons drawn from their own experiences: based on violence and often feature inferior writing.
3. The author wants readers to judge each book individually.

Say What?   **page 7**
1. underestimated
2. stripes
3. metal detectors
4. unparalleled
5. distinguished
6. milestone
7. interacting
8. preparedness
9. city

The Generals of the Sierra Nevada   **page 8**
1. to entertain young people while informing them
2. to inform professionals
3. to persuade citizens to take action
4. Opening 2
5. Opening 1
6. Opening 3

Tsunami Dangers   **page 10**
Student answers or summaries on this page will vary in wording, but should include the important points mentioned in the examples provided here.
1. This tsunami killed more than 2,000 people and destroyed villages along four miles of the coastline.
2. Earthquakes, volcanoes, and undersea avalanches might cause tsunami.
3. Scientists believe that residents along these coasts face danger from tsunami because terraces of loose sediment line these coasts. This loose sediment could avalanche, causing a tsunami.
4. Predicting undersea landslides before they happen will give coastal residents more time to evacuate.

5. Tsunami can kill coastal residents and destroy coastal communities. Scientists discovered that undersea avalanches can cause tsunami and that terraces of loose sediment line the Southern California and mid-Atlantic communities. They are searching for ways to predict these avalanches, so that they can evacuate coastal residents before a tsunami hits.

Chewy Doesn't Go to Yellowstone   **page 11**
1. Students might list any two of these ways pets might disturb the natural area or the wildlife or might offer other logical possibilities: Pets might eat or trample plants; chase, fight, or kill wildlife; spread disease to other animals; or poop.
2. Students might list any one of these possible ways pets might disturb other park visitors, as well as offering another logical possibility: Pets might bark, damage campsites, poop, or bite.
3. Students might list any two of these ways pets might become endangered, as well as offering other logical possibilities: Pets might get lost, eat poisonous plants, contract illnesses, be eaten, or fight other animals.
4. P
5. P

(Not) Just the Facts   **page 12**

1. F	5. F	9. O	13. O
2. O	6. F	10. F	14. O*
3. F	7. F	11. O	15. F
4. F	8. O	12. O	16. O*

(*Weather predictions are opinions of meteorologists.)

Have a Bug Feast   **page 14**
1. ME
2. ME
3. NME
4. NME (Hint: Ground-up insects could fit under either heading.)
5. Student answers will differ, but should include some variation or restatement of the following mutually exclusive categories:
Title A: Foods that Accidentally or Unavoidably Include Insects
Title B: Foods that Intentionally Include Insects

My Most Embarrassing Moment   **page 15**
Student answers will vary, as students voice some of these ideas in their own words.
1. The author started by setting the scene so that readers might more easily visualize the funny moment/could visualize where the girl and boy were seated in relationship to each other/could imagine themselves in the scene.
2. The author wanted readers to know how important this moment was to the girl so that her embarrassment would have more impact/so that readers could imagine her feelings.
3. The author uses repetition to build tension/build the expectation that something was going to happen/keep readers' attention/trick readers into believing that they could predict what would happen next.
4. Students might state that the author created surprise and humor when events turned out differently than expected.

Spacey Diets   page 16

1 tropical punch
1 lemonade
1 orange-pineapple drink
1 dried beef
1 shrimp cocktail
1 carrot sticks
1 peach ambrosia
3 beefsteak
2 macaroni and cheese

1 potatoes au gratin
1 broccoli au gratin
1 green beans with mushrooms
1 green beans and broccoli
1 butter cookies
1 chocolate pudding
1 tapioca pudding
3 candy-coated peanuts

Ocean Solutions   page 18

1. Students would cross out the letters that are crossed out below:

T	H	E	D	Y	P̷	I	N	G
P	L	A	N	T	L̷	S	W	O
S̷	R̷	E̷	T̷	S̷	A̷	F̷	U	L
D	E̷	C	A	I̷	N̷	R	R	Y
E	X	K̷	R̷	C	K̷	E	S	S
C	A	O̷	A̷	R	T̷	B	O	N
D	N̷	I	O	M̷	O̷	X	I	D
E	T	O	T	H	N̷	E	O	C
W̷	O̷	R̷	C̷	E	A	N	F	L
O	O	R	X	V	A	C	K	Y

2. The dying plants would carry excess carbon dioxide to the ocean floor.
3. Iron makes plankton grow faster.
4. Students would circle "Iron makes plankton grow faster."

Teasing Out the Answers   page 19

Brainteaser # 1: There are 7 people: a grandfather, a grandmother, a father, a mother, and three children.
Brainteaser #2: Monday
Brainteaser #3: Yes

Spend, Spend, Spend   page 20

1. Students might list specific retail or content sites that appeal to teens, such as MP3, Delia's, etc. They might also list generic sites that might appeal to teens, such as a site that sells clothes for teens, a site related to music for teens, etc.
2. 7 circles

> You're the best! You know it and we do, too. To prove it, we're putting your photo on your very own prepaid card. Sign up this week and we'll even load your card with $25.00 for your first purchase.
>
> Buy what you want with your own SpendBigBukz Prepaid Card. Your parents preload the account and you spend the money. The card works just like cash. What could be easier? Plus, you get cash back for every purchase you make. The more you spend, the more you earn!
>
> Be the best! Get a SpendBigBukz Prepaid Card now.

3. Within one week: $25.00 toward the first purchase. At any time, any two of the following: cash back for each purchase, easy purchases, a photo on the card, and the

4. Students might list any two of the following questions as well as additional ones that occur to the student: How much cash back is returned with each purchase? What happens if the card is lost or stolen? Does the prepaid card have maximum or minimum limits? What is the interest rate?

Tramp Art   page 22

Student drawings will vary.

Snoopy Snakes   page 23

Students will place brackets as follows: one set around the first three-sentence paragraph, another around the second and third paragraphs, and a third around the final paragraph.

Student answers to the question that follows the article will differ, but might include variations of the following ideas: Both the opening and the conclusion use short, snappy sentences. Both the opening and the conclusion use surprising statements. Both the opening and the conclusion use the word "robot."

Dreaming Up a Good Grade   page 24

Readers will circle various details that they find supportive of the main idea.
1. Two
2. Dr. Robert Stickgold
3. ⅔
4. The hippocampus

Mathew Brady's Plan to End Warfare   page 26

1. The daguerreotype process required them to sit perfectly still for three to fifteen minutes.
2. The invention of the photograph made on paper caused Mathew Brady to think that he could change history. Photographs required less exposure time, so that Brady could capture images of national life.
3. The end of the Civil War meant that people lost interest in his Civil War photographs. He could not sell the photographs he had spent so much to obtain, and he went bankrupt.
4. Student answers might differ, but might include any two of the following:
   The invention of the photograph on paper
   The shorter exposure time required by the invention of the photograph on paper
   Mathew Brady's interest in creating a record of national life
   Mathew Brady's ability to assemble a corps of photographers
   Mathew Brady's drive and ambition

Driving Distracted   page 28

Missing details include the following:
The top right portion of the concept map:
New Distractions
On-board Maps
Fax Machines
Wireless Access to the Internet

The bottom of the concept map:
New Laws Needed, Setting Limits for Devices

A New Capitol for a New Nation   page 29

Students will circle *melting pot*, *Like its flag*, and *Renaissance man*.
Student metaphors will differ.

The Capitol Building — page 30

1. Students might choose from among the following similarities: Both Thornton's original drawing and the completed Capitol Building feature domes, arched windows, columns, and wings extending out from either side of the domed central section. Students might notice other similarities.
2. Students might choose from among the following differences: Thornton's original drawing included a porch with a pointed roof in the central section, while the completed Capitol Building did not. The completed building includes stairs flanking either side of the dome, while Thornton's original drawing did not. Thornton's dome was a simple dome, while the completed Capitol Building features a high dome with columns and a cupola. Other than the dome, Thornton's original drawing featured a flat roof, while the completed Capitol Building reveals crowning structures on the roof. The completed Capitol Building features a statue on top of the cupola, while Thornton's drawing did not. Students might notice other differences.

Banana Vaccinations — page 31

Student answers will differ. They should give their opinions of a plan to modify bananas genetically so that they protect children against childhood illnesses, perhaps giving possible advantages. This serves as an original opinion that can be tested or refined after reading the article.

page 32

1. Students might mention any two of these advantages: Offering banana immunizations would be less painful, would not require refrigeration in isolated areas, would not require trained medical personnel to be present in isolated areas, would ultimately be cheaper in developing countries, would save lives of newborns and children, or would be more available in developing countries. Students might mention other advantages. Students might mention any two of the following drawbacks: it might be difficult to obtain financing for the project, many scientists or governments might be skeptical of the project, bananas are difficult to modify, dosages might be difficult to deliver with consistency, tolerance for disease might develop if dosages are not consistent, and modified banana trees would have to be kept separate from other plants. Students might mention other drawbacks.
2. The author offered a balanced viewpoint of banana vaccinations, because the author offered both advantages and possible drawbacks.
3. Students answers will differ, but should include at least two supporting facts from the article.

A Jungle Palace — page 33

Student-developed travel brochure opening paragraphs will differ, but should include some of the following specific details: the 170-room Maya palace of three stories was built sometime between A.D. 250 to A.D. 900, and featured 11 palace courtyards. The complex includes no temples or relics of war.

A Letter to Mike — page 34

1. Students can make this determination by looking up the year in which the Cuban Missile Crisis occurred, or by identifying the year in which Elvis Presley's song "Suspicion" first debuted.
2. Brenda mentions that her town is a refinery town and also that her town lies somewhere along the Gulf (of Mexico) coast. Students might also mention that her school practiced drills in case of a bombing, but that detail would be less precise, since schools across a broader geographical area might have practiced drills.
3. Yes
   No, because looking at a map could not narrow down the specific refinery town in which Brenda lived.

Spacewalk Drills — page 35

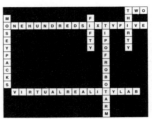

Vacation by Computer — page 37

1. the calendar
2. to the "sports and recreation" section of the heading or using the "Search for" function. Some students might also look at the calendar to see if any games were listed for the dates the family would be visiting.
3. the "hotel" section of the heading, the "Best for Kids" section, or the "Visitor's Guide" section
   Some students might also mention looking for hotels under the "Search for" function.
4. the "movies" section of the heading
5. the "maps" section of the heading or the "movies" section may include maps to each theater

Mapping It Out — page 38

1. Yes, it would be possible to drive from Dallas-Ft. Worth to Breckenridge.
2. Retrace the distance traveled on Rt. 180 by returning to I-20. Go west on I-20 to Putnam. Go north on Rt. 283 to Albany. Turn east on Rt. 180 to Breckenridge.

Supplying Electricity — page 40

1. Students might choose any four of the following details: scientists predicted that most of us would live in solar-powered homes by the turn of the twenty-first century, scientists believed that solar energy would power many devices, solar energy produces less pollution, solar-powered appliances cost less to run, scientists' predictions fell short, solar-powered homes cost more to build, few people wanted to spend the money to build solar-powered homes.
2. Students would choose A, the wall that is topped by the words "Solar cells prove more beneficial to third-world countries than to developed countries."

The Irish Famine — page 41

Student answers will differ, but they might jot down some of the following details:
The *Swan* set sail from Cork, Ireland.
The *Swan* set sail May 1, 1848.
The *Swan* carried victims of the Irish Famine.
The *Swan* sailed toward America.
Cholera often killed as many as ⅓ of the passengers.
Irish families often subdivided their farms.
Potatoes could be grown on small lots.
Potatoes supplied most nutritional needs.
Most families grew the same varieties of potatoes.
Blight was accidentally introduced into the country in 1845.
Crops died year after year.
The Irish famine was the worst European famine in the 1800s.
After the famine, farmers tried new methods and crops.
After the famine, the Irish varied their diet.

In 1844 Ireland's population was about 8,400,000.
By 1851 more than one million would be dead.
By 1851 a million and a half Irish would have emigrated to
    North America and Britain.

High-Tech Plastic Swimming Pools   page 42
Students should put a check beside #4, "Necessity is the mother of invention."

Golden Words   page 44
1. Student answers might differ, but most will conclude that the author might have wanted to implant the idea that Greenhow was wild or wayward, even from childhood.
2. Student answers might differ, but most will conclude that the author might have wanted readers to believe that Greenhow's own actions contributed to her death.
3. Most students will conclude that the author wanted readers to feel that Greenhow's impulsiveness and waywardness led to her own death. They will use the author's introduction of the nickname "Wild Rose" and the drowning caused by the weight of the gold as evidence of the author's bias. Students might draw other conclusions, as long as they support those conclusions with valid points from the article.

An fMRI for Your Thoughts   page 45
Student answers will differ. The following is an example of a paraphrase of the main points of the article:

An fMRI uses sound waves to form images of a functioning or working body. By determining where blood flows in the brain, scientists can tell which parts of the brain are most active when a volunteer experiences certain sensations or emotions. They can study the thinking brain. This kind of study may prepare scientists to help people who have suffered brain injuries.

Secret Pal   page 46
It appears that each family member sent a card.

Mummies Have No Secrets   page 48
1. Student titles will vary, but should include some variation on the titles "Bone Group" and "Organs, Wrappings, and Artifacts Group" or "Everything But Bone Group."
2. The mummies could be classified in the following manners: by century in which they lived, by gender, by age at death, or by social category to which they belonged.

Welcome to Life as a Cyborg!   page 50
1. Students might list any of the following words: *interesting, helpful, enthusiastic, out* of *sorts, cranky, happy,* or *unhappy.*
2. An exaggeration
3. A deliberate understatement.
4. sarcasm/satire
5. Most students will conclude that the author wanted students to believe that it was weird or inadvisable to think of implanting chips into a human body.
6. Student answers will differ.

Virus Killers   page 51
1. F   4. F
2. F   5. F
3. O   6. F

The Old Days Weren't Like You Thought   page 52
Students will offer differing generalizations before reading the article, but after finishing it, should refine their generalizations, concluding that prehistoric people wore finely woven cloths and that women contributed more to those prehistoric societies than was previously thought.

What's This?   pages 53 and 54
These are Chinese calligraphy writing tools. Student answers will differ on these questions, as they are asked to draw an original conclusion, then refine that conclusion with each clue provided. The original conclusion might be an illogical one or one that is clearly wrong. This exercise concentrates more on refining skills than on drawing the correct conclusion immediately.

Al Capp and an American Tradition   page 55
Students will put check marks beside the following statements:
1. Caplin began to draw cartoons after losing his leg in a trolley accident.
2. In Al Capp's cartoon, a character called Sadie Hawkins chased the men, looking for a likely husband.
3. "Li'l Abner" was introduced during the Depression, when Americans needed a reason to laugh.
4. In the late 1930s, women did not often chase men.

Bacteria Eat Toxic Waste   page 56
1. d   3. a
2. c   4. c

Curious Animals   page 58
1. Curious animals explore their environment, developing knowledge of the environment and new motor skills.
2. Pavlov's experiments explored conditioning.
3. Students might choose any three of the following: conditioning, trial and error, latent learning, imprinting, play or curiosity, or insight.
4. No, young toads and other amphibians do not appear to play.

Infections in Space   page 59
1. The Mir space station was probably used for an extended period of time.
2. The longer space travel lasts, the more microorganisms grow inside a spacecraft.
3. Known medications probably would not be very useful against the mutated microorganisms astronauts might encounter in space.

Previewing the Past   page 60
1. b
2. a
3. a
4. a
5. b. *Life without electricity presented special challenges.*

Rabid Vampires   page 62
Student answers would differ, but would include any five of the following similarities:

Rabies
Most are male.
Victims have bloody mouths.
Many victims in Poland, Russia, and Hungary.
Epidemics spread in the late 1600s and again in 1721-1728.
Victims bite others.
Victims suffer facial contortions.
Restlessness causes victims to wander at night.
Strong light, mirrors, or odors trigger facial spasms.
Victims look lifelike after death.

Vampires
Most are male.
Vampires have bloody mouths.
Students might discover other similarities.

Many myths about vampires in Poland, Russia, and Hungary.
Myths spread in the late 1600s and and again in 1721-1728.
Vampires bite others.
Vampires change shape.
Vampires walk at night.
Vampires fear sunlight, mirrors, and garlic.
Vampires are said to live after death.
2. Most students would conclude that Gomez-Alonso's theory is reasonable and would list some of the above similarities as support for their conclusions.

Jimmy's Vow — page 63
Students would put check marks beside statements 2 and 3.

Short and Snappy — page 64
1. Alka-Seltzer's slogan is short, uses repetition, rhyme, and/or a rhythmic meter.
2. American Telephone and Telegraph's slogan is a short command that appeals to sentiment.
3. Campbell's Condensed Soups' slogan is short and uses alliteration or repetition.
4. Chevrolet's slogan is short, and uses rhyme and a rhythmic meter.
5. Hellman's Mayonnaise slogan is short, has a rhythmic meter, and uses snob appeal.
6. Ace Hardware Stores' slogan is short, uses rhyme, alliteration, and a rhythmic meter. Some students might feel that it also appeals to everyone, since everyone feels in need of help at times.
7. Pepsi-Cola's slogan is a short command that has snob appeal.
8. Pepsodent Toothpaste's slogan uses rhyme and a rhythmic meter. Some students might also feel that it uses humor.

Student-written slogans will differ, but should relate to the school name and should use at least one of these tactics: a short length, alliteration or rhyme, a rhythmic meter, an appeal to everyone or snob appeal, a command, or humor or sentiment.

Candlestick Charts — page 66
1. The last price of the day would have been higher than the first price of the trading day. Anyone selling CDs would be likely to receive an even higher price the next trading day.
2. On the next trading day, the student would likely be buying extra CDs rather than selling the ones on hand, since prices were likely to be lower the next day.
3. On this trading day, the price zoomed up above the opening price, then fell back, so that prices were at their lowest at the close of the trading day.
4. Sometime after trading opened, prices dropped below the first price of the day, but then they climbed again, so that prices were at their highest at the close of the trading day.

Song and Culture Go Together — page 67
Student answers will differ, as the student will be comparing Tuva throat-singers to a favorite singing star or group.

Tracking Down a Friend — page 69
Matt left the gift.

Nissen Gets a Job — page 70
Students will underline the following words or phrases: *carries, claims, seen, collecting, supposed, collapse, used, possess,* and *imagination.*

Doctor Anna — page 72
1. Students might state that the author appeared to admire Doctor Anna's intelligence and persistence.
2. Student answers will differ, according to the answer given

to the first question, but might support their answers by mentioning the author's depiction of Doctor Anna's struggle to get into medical school and then to find the cause of milk sickness; the author's use of the loaded words *curiosity, determination, famous,* and *silly ideas;* the author's use of a narrative format that helps readers identify with Doctor Anna; or the mention of Abraham Lincoln's mother's death of milk sickness, helping readers to understand the importance of Doctor Anna's work.
3. Students might state that the author probably holds the unstated belief that women should not have endured such difficulties attending medical school in the early nineteenth century, or that they deserved to attend medical school.
4. It was Doctor Anna's viewpoint that these ideas were silly.

Young Inventors — page 73
1. F
2. F
3. O
4. O
5. F

Your Turn to Be an Intern — page 74
Student answers will differ.

Digging Up the Twenty-First Century — page 76
Student answers will differ but should include evidence that they look beyond the known and accepted uses of an athletic shoe, a poster of a band, or a beanbag chair.

Mapping Out a Fortune — page 77
1. narrative
2. comparing and contrasting
3. comparing and contrasting
4. narrative

E-mail Alert — page 78
1. According to the alert, David McDavid is a U.S. Representative.
2. According to the alert, Ronald Sneed is an attorney from Omaha, Nebraska.
3. The article does not identify the source of the information about Bill 409.
4. Student answers might include the following suggestions:
Do an Internet search to verify that U.S. Representative David McDavid exists.
Do an Internet search to verify that an attorney named Ronald Sneed works in Omaha, Nebraska, or check the Yellow Pages from a large urban library's collection of Yellow Pages from various cities.
Do an Internet search to verify that Bill 409 exists.
Check the U.S. Postal Service's site to find information about e-mail surcharges, or phone a local post office manager to inquire about the surcharges.
Do a global Internet search using keywords from the article.
Look in the phone book for the name of the student's U.S. Representative and call the local office, asking about Bill 409.
Check with the Internet service provider to find out if the mail is a hoax.
5. Most students would conclude that the proposed surcharge does not seem logical, because people would rebel at paying for a formerly free service or because it would prove too difficult to collect the surcharge.
6. Most students would conclude that Bill 409 does not exist and that the e-mail promotes a hoax or urban legend.

Working It Out   page 80
1. Students will put X's on all tables, except 113, 120, 125, and 170.
2. 125, Kris
3. 120, Matt
4. 170, Katie
5. 113, Elana

War of the Dictionaries   page 82
Most students would conclude that language should be fixed to some degree so that people could communicate with each other more easily, but that new words related to new technology must also be included.

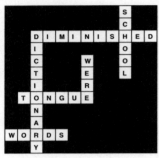

Make This   page 83
Students will circle the origami kimono.

Working Canines   page 84
1. Dogs sometimes have behavior problems that send them to pounds or shelters.
2. One solution is to occupy dogs with tasks appropriate to their breeds.
3. Student answers will differ, but they might mention some of the following details:
Nicky, a German shepherd, landed in a pound because he was too hyperactive.
Nicky worked productively and happily when given the task of searching ships for contraband.
People and dogs have worked together 10,000-20,000 years.
Dogs work as entertainers, in search and rescue, in herding and hunting, and assisting police and military units.
A retriever's high energy makes it a good dog for serving people with disabilities or retrieving game.
A border collie's intelligence helps it herd.

Archeologists Working Here   page 85
1. Student answers will differ as they delineate their prior knowledge and impressions about the working conditions for archeologists, but from the illustration, they should draw some conclusions about the harshness of working in some environments.
2. Student-created questions will differ, but should relate to the working conditions of archeologists.

Not Just Poking Around   page 86
1. Student answers will differ, depending on whether their student-created questions from page 85 were answered by reading the article.
2. Student answers about the two new things learned by reading the article will differ, depending on their prior knowledge of the working conditions of archeologists.

A Scary Business   page 88
1. The two doctors began the business because they could not find the models of human skeletons they needed to teach their students.

2. Producing torsos from which blood could be drawn had the effect of allowing medical and rescue personnel to practice emergency procedures. Some students might extrapolate that lives were saved as a result.
3. The limitation on the trade of human bones caused the two doctors to experience difficulty finding bones to cast. Some students might mention that this caused them to ask a dentist to join the business and that the limitation also caused them financial difficulties.
4. effect, cause
5. cause, effect
6. cause, effect
7. effect, cause

No Apple a Day   page 90
1. **Rehydrated foods:** d, dried foods to which water is added before eating.
Thermostabilized foods: a, canned foods that have been heated to keep them from spoiling.
Intermediate-moisture foods: b, partially dried foods to which no water is added before eating.
Natural foods: c, foods eaten in their natural form.
2. T
3. N
4. N
5. IM
6. R
7. Carrots most likely were included on the first day's menu, since they could not be frozen or refrigerated and might spoil by the eighth day.

Mind Your (Animal) Manners   page 91
1. Most students will conclude that scientists did not always understand that animals had culture. The statement that *Scientists are discovering that animals have culture, too,* hints at a time when scientists did not believe that animals had culture.
2. The author concludes that animal culture is learned.
3. Most students will conclude that culture helps smooth relationships between the animals in a group, just as it does with humans. Students might note that in order to draw this conclusion, they assumed that animals do have culture and that the different members of a group recognize gestures or other facets of animal culture.

Dog Manners   page 92
The puzzle will spell out the sentence *To show a readiness to play, dogs bow with their heads down and their front legs outstretched.*

They Can't Help It   page 94
1. Firstborn students might write: Firstborns tend to want things to go smoothly. They tend to be authoritarian, bossy, and respectful of authority. Students might add that firstborns tend to be leaders of socially acceptable reforms.
Middleborn students might write: Middleborns tend to be good at refereeing or easing cooperation between groups.
Laterborn students might write: Laterborns tend to be tolerant, open to new ideas, and ready to begin new movements.
Students also will list at least one way in which they do not fit the generalization for people of their birth order.
2. V
3. I
4. V
5. I
6. V
7. families during the Depression of the 1930s
8. firstborns

9. laterborns
10. firstborns

Cookie Spies   page 95
1. MadeUpCompany l   6. T
2. Both companies   7. T
3. Both companies   8. F
4. Neither company   9. F
5. T

Practice, Practice   page 97
1. a   4. a
2. b   5. b
3. b   6. a

Pig Transplants   page 98
1. Student answers should mention that the author did not want to draw sympathy for the animals or that the author did not want to poison readers against the idea of using animal transplants to save human lives.
2. The author presents unbalanced writing, because the author left out an important consideration when thinking about using animal transplants to save human lives. The author did not give readers all the sides of an argument.

They Already Know Your Name   page 99
Student summaries will differ, but should state most of the following ideas:
Much personal information is available to retailers, insurance companies, pharmacies, and other companies and people. Measures to protect privacy include refusing permission to schools to release personal information, avoiding filling out Internet surveys or contest forms, or avoiding telephone surveys, among other tactics.

                                                           page 100
Subject: charge on credit card
Name of Company You Are Complaining About: *Anazm Marketing*
Address of Company: *not available*
Company Web Site: *not available*
Company E-Mail Address: *not available*
Company Phone Number: *not available*
How Did the Company Initially Contact You? *By telephone*
How Much Did the Company Ask You to Pay? *no fee mentioned*
How Did You Pay the Company? *By credit card*
How Much Did You Actually Pay the Company? *$59.93*
Name of Company Representative or Salesperson Who Contacted You: *not available*
Explain Your Problem: *A salesperson contacted me by telephone, without identifying herself as a salesperson, and asked if I wanted her to order a homecoming corsage. I was charged for the corsage but never received it.*

Student suggestions for locating the needed information might include any two of the following: look up Anazm Marketing in the telephone book, do an Internet search for Anazm Marketing, contact Better Business Bureau for information on Anazm Marketing, contact a local television station's consumer advocate for help, find out if the marketing and advertising industries have some kind of supervisory committees to which abuses might be reported, or other ideas that might occur to the student.

Genetic Basis of Behavior   page 101
Student answers will differ, but should include the following ideas: Some people believe that genes could control both physical traits and behavior. While some researchers like the idea that behavior might have a genetic basis, others worry about this idea. Their worries may be exaggerated.

Healing Hearts   page 103
1. N   3. N
2. D   4. N

Diligent Hero   page 104
testify: *give evidence*
transpired: *occurred*
diligence: *earnestness*
toiled: *worked*
sleuthing: *detective work*
persevered: *continued*
armed: *equipped*
documented: *provided a written account of*
achieved: *reached*

No Regrets for Esther Kim   page 106
1. Students might suggest that the author used a narrative form so that readers might more closely identify with the people or events described
2. Students might conclude that the author intended to create the effect that the readers were experiencing what Esther Kim experienced. The author might have wanted readers to feel more emotion.
3. Students might conclude that the author's unstated belief was that Esther Kim's decision was the only honorable decision or that it is better to sacrifice for a friend than to win for oneself.
4. Students might write something similar to one of the following statements: Esther Kim's sacrifice was foolish/Esther Kim's decision cheated her coaches and the other people who worked with her to achieve her success/It is more honorable to do one's best than to give up.
5. Most students would conclude that the purpose of this article was to encourage readers to share Esther Kim's experience. They could point to the narrative format, the use of loaded words such as *terrible* and *regret,* or the characterization of her decision as heroic or that of a champion. Some students might conclude that the author's purpose was to persuade readers to accept the belief that sacrificing for a friend is honorable. Those students might point to the statements that winning isn't everything and that Kim was a champion, as well as mentioning the author's unstated belief and bias. Although the main purpose was actually to encourage readers to share Kim's experience, students could argue for the other purpose as long as they support their ideas with these examples.

Life on Mars   page 108
1. Christopher P. McKay is the source of this information. Students might mention a need to know McKay's educational level, degree of acceptance from the scientific community, or publication history, among other suggestions.
2. The *Scientific American* included a discussion of McKay's theories. Students might mention a need to know the educational level of the magazine's staff and writers, its acceptance in the scientific community, and its history, among other suggestions.
3. It was someone else's theory that giant mirrors could be used to warm Mars' atmosphere. Most students would conclude that it would be impractical to transport giant mirrors to Mars.
4. McKay considers transporting small chemical factories to Mars to be the most workable method.
   Students might suggest a need to know the size and cost of the factories, or the number of factories needed, among other suggestions.

5. Students might conclude that many of the ideas McKay discusses seem unworkable.

The Many Lives of Grace Halsell   **page 110**
The illustrations should be numbered in the following order: 4, 1, 5, 2, 3.
On the following questions, students may draw different conclusions, but most will conclude the following:
1. Publishers might not have taken her ideas as seriously or might not have been as willing to consider publishing her book.
2. She would have published her books in a different order. The order of publication was probably not important.
3. If Griffin had not written his book until 1979, Halsell might not have thought of living as minority women until that time. She might have moved on to other activities and not had the time or inclination to pursue life as a minority woman after 1979.

A Hard Price   **page 111**
1. Student answers should include any two of the following ideas: Both Azmari musicians and European minstrels worked in the courts of the nobles of their societies; often could not read music; memorized and often improvised music; and used puns, satire, and humor to mock others.
2. Student answers should be a variation of the following concepts: *the reader, a modern student or musician, a student in a first band concert,* or *me.*

Some Things Never Change   **page 112**
1. Student answers should reflect that the author wanted to achieve an easy, conversational voice, and that the less formal *you* and the present-tense verbs help to establish that voice.
2. The author probably intended to create the feeling that the Internet could be fun.
   Supporting details might include any of the following: the narrative opening, the informal or conversational voice, and the lack of specific details about the types of Web sites or services mentioned. After reading this article, the student does not have enough information to contact the Web sites mentioned or to gauge their cost or reliability.

Virtual Schools   **page 114**
1. b   5. c
2. b   6. a
3. a   7. b
4. c

Sky-High Dreams   **page 115**
Students will place three sets of brackets as follows: one set around the first paragraph of the selection, another set that encloses the second-through-fourth paragraphs, and a third set that encloses the final paragraph.

page 116
1. Students might conclude that the author probably believed that seventh and eighth graders would be more interested in Fred Parks if they could first imagine him as someone like themselves.
2. Students will circle *Dreams can stir people to overcome obstacles and achieve much.*
3. The third paragraph reveals that Parks again needed to draw from his vision or dreams if he was going to overcome the obstacles encountered when he tried to convince reluctant city governments to use the Aerobus system.

4. In the conclusion, the author states that Parks finally found a city to adopt the Aerobus system, and that in his mid-90s Parks still possessed the same vision he had possessed when he was a young boy. Parks' dreams helped him overcome the obstacles he faced when he tried to find a city to adopt his plan. This relates to the theme that dreams help one overcome obstacles.

Gesture That Again?   **page 117**
Students will number the paragraphs in the following order: 4, 5, 2, 3

An American Icon   **page 118**
Students will label the building on the right side of the page "Flatiron Building," and will label the building on the left side of the page "Reliance Building."

The Tale of an Ancient Sailor   **page 120**
1. F   8. F
2. F   9. O
3. O   10. O
4. F   11. F
5. F   12. O
6. O   13. F
7. F   14. F
                15. O